STUDENT BOOK

Mc Graw Hill Education

ELLevate
ENGLISH TEEN

mheducation.com

Copyright © 2016 by McGraw-Hill Education.

Published by McGraw-Hill Education.

ISBN: 978-0-07-717957-1

LEVEL 2 — Scope and Sequence

Unit	Unit Theme	⚙ Grammar	🎧 Listening
Theme Question Units 1-3: How are we alike and different?			
1	Home, Sweet Home	*Wh-* Question Words; *Want to*	Listen for specific information
2	Celebrations	Simple Present of the verb *Be* in Yes / No Questions; Count and Noncount Nouns with *some / any / a / an*	Identify main ideas
3	Daily Lives	Questions with *How often*; Adverbs of Frequency; *Know how to* vs *Learn how to*	Listen for time words and phrases
	Use What You Know Units 1–3		
Theme Question Units 4-6: How does the past shape us?			
4	Time	Regular and Irregular Verbs in the Simple Past; Intensifiers	Predict from pictures
5	Now and Then	*There was / There were*; Indefinite Pronouns	Put events in order
6	Giving Advice	*Used to*; *Should / Shouldn't*	Connect main ideas and good titles
	Use What You Know Units 4–6		
Theme Question Units 7-9: What can we learn through traveling?			
7	Travel	*Should / Why don't you . . . ?*; *Let's*; *Have to / Had to*; *Go* + verb + *ing*	Listen for specific ideas: Causes
8	Collections	Possessive Pronouns; Pronouns: *One / Ones*; *Too* + adjective	Listen for specific information
9	Transportation	Comparatives; Spelling Changes; Superlatives	Listen for main ideas: Speaker's purpose
	Use What You Know Units 7–9		
Theme Question Units 10-12: How can we help each other?			
10	Offering and Giving Help	*Will* for future; *Be going to* to express future	Listen for the main ideas
11	Requests	*Can / Could* and *Will / Would* to express possibility; *Want / Tell / Ask* for requests; *Let / Will* to show intentions	Make an indirect request or suggestion
12	Stories	Present Perfect; Present Perfect vs Simple Past	Infer the reasons for situations or actions
	Use What You Know Units 10–12		

🎤 Pronunciation	💬 Speaking	📖 Reading	✏️ Writing
Intonation with *Wh-* Questions	Ask questions for information	Read for specific information	Use specific details
Intonation in Yes / No Questions	Decline an invitation	Read for the main idea	Add specific details
Sentence Stress with Adverbs of Frequency	Expressions that tell *"how often"*	Read for specific time phrases	Write clear schedules
Informal speaking: *Don't* and *Didn't*	Indicate time	Read for causes and effects	Use time expressions
Informal speaking: Final *t* in *wasn't* and *weren't*	Give reasons	Make predictions from pictures	Write topic sentences
The voiced and unvoiced *th-* sound	Give suggestions	Write titles and headings	Write an email to give advice to a friend
Word Stress	Ask people to repeat slowly	Read for specific ideas: Causes	Write a postcard
Short *a*, long *a*, *-r* controlled *a*, *-l* controlled *a*	Describe objects and ownership	Read for specific ideas: Nouns	Write descriptions
Final *-th*	Agree and disagree	Read for main ideas: Author's purpose	Write concluding sentences
Silent *-t*	Show support and offer help	Read for the main idea	Plan a paragraph
Short *o* vs long *o*	Make direct requests	Make a request through inference	Make a formal request
Informal speaking: *was*	Show interest and check that you understand	Infer the author's intentions	Write a short story

1 | Home, Sweet Home

2 | Celebrations

3 | Daily Lives

How are we alike and different?

 Look at the picture. Read the unit topics and answer the questions.

- **How are these people alike?**
- **How are these people different?**
- **How are these people like you?**

CAN DO statements

After the next three units, you will be able to . . .

- describe your home.
- compare different celebrations.
- describe a day in your life.

In this unit, I will learn to . . .
- describe my home.
- ask questions using *Wh-* question words.
- listen and read for specific information.

1 | **Get Ready**

 What makes a good home?

A. Look at the pictures. How are the homes different? Read each description.

This home is in Panama. Long poles hold up the home over the water. It has **windows** with a view of both land and sea.

Homes in cities such as Hong Kong are small. Many homes are in tall apartment buildings.

This is a home in India. It has colorful **walls** and a blue door.

This large home in Thailand has two levels. The front door welcomes guests, and the windows look out over the trees and plants.

B. Read the sentences and circle T for *True* or F for *False*.

1. The apartment buildings are in a large city in Thailand.   T   (F)

2. The home in Hong Kong is on a beach.   T   (F)

3. There are two levels in the home in India.   T   (F)

4. The home in Panama has windows.   (T)   F

5. The home in the sea is on long poles.   (T)   F

6. The front door welcomes guests to the large house in India.   (T)   F

7. The home in Thailand has windows with a view of trees and plants.   (T)   F

Pair and Share

With a partner, ask and answer these questions.

Which home do you like the most?

I like the home. *ho is my*

Ask and answer this question about your home.

What do you like about your home?

I like *everithing*

A. Listen to the audio and read along. Guess the meaning of the words in bold.

Homes around the world may look **different**, but they are all the **same**. Most homes have bedrooms where people sleep. The bedrooms often have a **closet** to store **clothing** and shoes. Most have a living room where a family **gathers** to relax. A **kitchen** is another important room where a family **prepares** food. Some homes have a separate room for eating called a **dining room**. A bathroom helps the family keep clean. Homes also have **walls** that separate rooms and give **privacy**, and **windows** so that sunlight can **warm** the home.

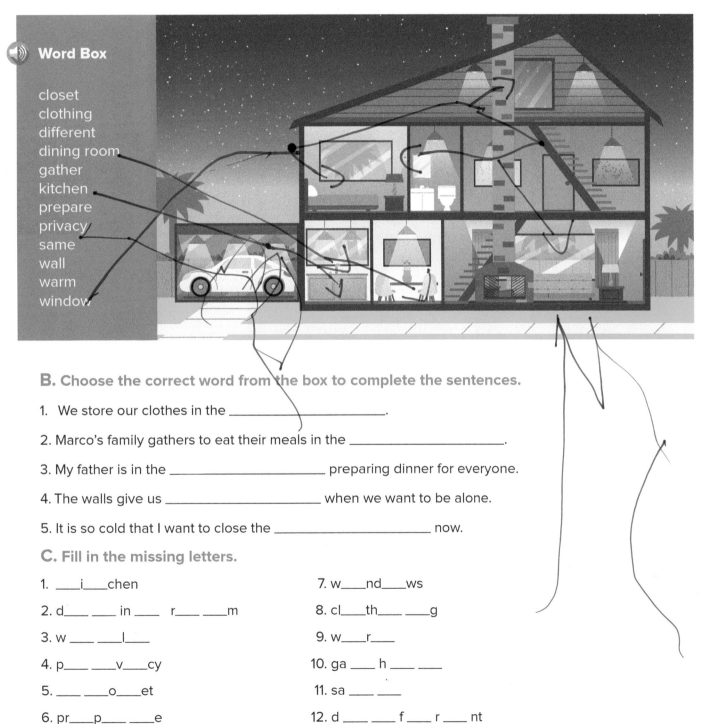

Word Box

closet
clothing
different
dining room
gather
kitchen
prepare
privacy
same
wall
warm
window

B. Choose the correct word from the box to complete the sentences.

1. We store our clothes in the _____.

2. Marco's family gathers to eat their meals in the _____.

3. My father is in the _____ preparing dinner for everyone.

4. The walls give us _____ when we want to be alone.

5. It is so cold that I want to close the _____ now.

C. Fill in the missing letters.

1. ____i____chen

2. d____ ____ in ____ r____ ____m

3. w ____ ____l____

4. p____ ____v____cy

5. ____ ____o____et

6. pr____p____ ____e

7. w____nd____ws

8. cl____th____ ____g

9. w____r____

10. ga ____ h ____ ____

11. sa ____ ____

12. d ____ ____ f ____ r ____ nt

Wh- **Question Words**

Questions are asked to get information. They often begin with a question word such as *Who, What, Which, Where, When, Why,* and *How.*

Question Word	What does it ask about?	Example
Who	a person	**Who** is she?
What	a thing	**What** are you eating?
Which	a choice	**Which** home is your favorite?
Where	a place	**Where** is your school?
When	a time	**When** is lunch?
Why	a reason	**Why** are Maria and Simon leaving school?
How	a condition	**How** are you feeling today?

For grammar reference, go to Grammar Appendix.

A. Look at the pictures. Read and answer the questions.

Who is she?

Where is this?

What time is it?

B. Complete the sentences using *Wh-* question words.

1. _Where_ is your friend's house?

2. _____ is your soccer game?

3. _Where_ is Yamini smiling?

4. _What_ apartment building is yours?

5. _What_ is your mother cooking for dinner?

6. _Where_ is your family going for the holiday?

7. _What_ is your room different than mine?

8. _Who_ is your best friend?

9. _Why_ is the window closed?

10. _What_ color is your bedroom?

C. Put the words in order to make questions.

1. are / When / leaving / we

When we are leaving ?

2. in / the living room / What / is

What is in the living ? room

3. is / Where / the remote control

Where is the remote control ?

4. doing / is / How / John

How is John doing ?

5. go to / can / the museum / Who

Who can go to the museum ?

6. he / Why / is / his room / cleaning / not

Why he is not cleaning ? this room?

Want to

Want to means "wish for something" or "desire something."

Use an infinitive, *to* + verb, after the verb *want*.

I *want to* go to bed.

You *want to* brush your teeth.

She *wants to* buy some fruit.

We *want to* live in this house.

They *want to* watch TV in the living room.

Where is she?
She is at the supermarket. She *wants to* buy strawberries.

D. Rewrite the sentences using *want to*.

1. I wish to go home at 8 p.m.

I want to go home at 8 p.m

2. She and her mother wish to cook at home.

She and her mother want to cook at home

3. Rina wishes to paint her bedroom.

Rina want to paint he bedroom

4. They desire to move into a bigger home.

They want to move into a bigger home

5. He desires to move to Tokyo.

He want to move to Tokyo

6. Jason and I wish to buy a house near the park.

Jason and I want to buy a house near the park.

Pair and Share

With a partner, ask *Wh-* questions using **When, Where, What, Who, How,** and **Why.**

Which is the biggest country in the world?

The biggest country is . Russia

When is your best friend's birthday?

It's . I dont no

E. Write two sentences about things you wish for using *want to*.

1. _I want to know speack english._

2. _I want to pass in year 7._

4 | Listening 🎧

Before Listening

A. Look at the pictures. Would you like to live in a house like this? Why or why not?

 B. Listen to the audio. Answer the questions. Listen again to check your answers.

1. What is the house compared to? _____

2. What year was the home built? _____

3. Where is the house? _____

4. Why is this home a good idea for someone who likes trees? _____

5. What makes the rooms warm and bright? _____

After Listening

C. What kind of house would you like to live in? Share with a partner.

5 | Pronunciation 🎤

Intonation with *Wh-* Questions

Listen carefully. Is the sentence asking a question? Intonation falls on the last word of a *wh-* question.

A. Listen. Circle R for *rising intonation* or F for *falling intonation* of the last word.

1. R / F   2. R / F   3. R / F   4. R / F   5. R / F   6. R / F

B. Listen to the audio and repeat.

 A. Listen to the conversation and complete the sentences. Listen again to check your answers.

Bob: I just heard your family is moving into a new home. (1) _____ is your first night there?

Sally: Our first night will be Friday.

Bob: (2) _____ many rooms does it have?

Sally: Let's see. There are three bedrooms, one bathroom, a large living room, and a great kitchen.

Bob: (3) _____ is it like on the outside?

Sally: It's white and has a big tree in front of it.

Bob: Wow! (4) _____ is it?

Sally: It's on First Street, close to the park.

Bob: (5) _____ many minutes does it take to get to school?

B. Your Turn

Roleplay the conversation with a partner. Then, write Sally's response to Bob's last question.

Your idea: _____

_____

 C. Listen to the audio. Take notes to prepare for a conversation about a house you would like.

Pair and Share

With a partner, ask and answer *Wh-* questions about a house you would like to have.

What is it like?

It has three bedrooms, . . .

Where is it?

It is . . .

Reading Strategy:
Read for specific information

Identify your purpose for reading by previewing the title, photographs, and questions before reading. Then use these steps to find specific information as you read.

- Check the questions.
- Think about what information you need before reading.
- Read the text to find specific information.

Before Reading

A. Look at these pictures. How are these homes alike? How are they different?

B. Read the text. Underline key details about the different homes.

 There Is No Place Like Home

In parts of Mongolia, people move from place to place often. They move to find new land for grazing. They carry their homes, called yurts, with them. Yurts are light in weight. They are made in the shape of a circle, and then they are covered with thick mats. Yurts have one big room with no **walls**, so there is no **privacy**. When it is cold, people **gather** and build a fire in their yurt. A hole in the roof allows smoke to escape.

Those are not **windows** on the roof of this home. They look the same, but those are solar panels, which change energy from the sun into electricity. This brick house is very eco-friendly, which means it helps protect the environment. This two-story home does not harm the earth. The home needs to be in a place that receives a lot of sunlight.

A houseboat is a house built onto a boat. Houseboats can be small or large. Houseboats have different rooms, such as a **kitchen**, a **dining room**, and a **closet**. People can sleep and eat on the boat. If people on a houseboat do not like where they live, they can easily move to a different spot on the river or the sea.

After Reading

C. Complete the sentences based on the text.

1. People who live in a houseboat live on the ___sea___ or the ___water___.

2. Solar panels collect ___energy for houses___

3. Solar panels are usually placed on the ___top___ of a home.

4. The easiest home to move is the _____ because _____.

5. An eco-friendly home does not harm _____.

6. Homes with solar panels are built in _____.

D. Choose one house described in the text. Write two sentences that tell interesting details about the house.

_____

_____

8 | Writing

Writing Strategy:
Use specific details

A. What type of home would you like to live in? Tell your partner specific details about the home of your dreams.

Online surveys ask for specific details. Using specific details will help you find what you are looking for.
- Some online questions require a *yes* or *no* answer.
- Others might require the name of a place, a person, or a number.
- Information you give online may be shared with others. Always be careful!

B. Complete the online survey to search for your dream home. Use specific details to find the home you want.

Number of bedrooms:

_____

Number of bathrooms:

_____

Location: (city, country, beach, mountains, etc.)

_____

Type of house: (houseboat, yurt, apartment, mountain cabin, etc.)

_____

Outdoor features: (basketball court, pool, garden, etc.)

_____

Indoor features: (movie room, pool, game room, etc.)

_____

Write the specific details of your dream home in three to four sentences. _____

_____

_____

_____

UNIT 2 Celebrations

In this unit, I will learn to . . .
- talk about celebrations around the world.
- use the simple present of the verb *be* in yes / no questions.
- listen and read to identify the main idea.

1 | Get Ready

Why do people celebrate?

A. Look at the pictures. What are they celebrating? Read the passage.

Celebrating the Dead

Many countries have traditions to remember family members who have died.

In Mexico, families **celebrate** the Day of the Dead. They take flowers to a cemetery on November 1 and 2. Mexicans **decorate** a house altar with photographs, candles, flowers, and food.

During the Obon **festival** in Japan, people believe that their ancestors' spirits return to their homes to visit family. On the first day of Obon, people visit the cemetery and make a house altar. Obon is celebrated in July or August. At the end of the festival, people place floating lanterns in rivers and lakes to guide the spirits back.

Many countries celebrate Halloween on October 31. It is from an old **holiday** that honors the spirits of the dead. Today, children dress up in costumes and go house to house asking for candy. Some people **organize** a party.

B. Answer the questions.

1. What do these three festivals celebrate?

   _____

2. When do people celebrate these three festivals?

   _____

3. Where do people decorate house altars?

   _____

4. Why do people float lanterns on lakes and rivers?

   _____

5. In which festival do people wear costumes?

   _____

Pair and Share

With a partner, ask and answer questions about celebrations.

> What is your favorite celebration?

> I like to celebrate . . .

> What do people in your country celebrate in July?

> We celebrate . . .

A. Listen to the audio and read along. Guess the meaning of the words in bold.

My favorite national **holiday** is our **Independence Day** on July 4. It is the **birthday** of the United States. Every year, my family **organizes** a big **barbecue** at our home to **celebrate**. My father starts a fire and grills chicken or fish. We invite our neighbors and friends. Everyone brings a favorite food.

We **decorate** the yard with colorful banners and balloons. We place small **flags** on the table. We play baseball and other games. My school organizes a big **festival** where teachers and students participate. Like other holidays, such as Thanksgiving, **Christmas**, **Mother's Day**, and the **New Year**, everyone has a good time!

Word Box

barbecue	flag
birthday	holiday
celebrate	Independence Day
Christmas	Mother's Day
decorate	New Year
festival	organize

B. Match the words from the box with the correct definitions.

1. holiday	•	•	a piece of cloth with colors that represent a country
2. organize	•	•	an outdoor meal that people grill and eat
3. decorate	•	•	plan and arrange an activity
4. flag	•	•	a national holiday in the United States and other countries
5. barbecue	•	•	the day of the year that a person was born
6. Independence Day	•	•	a special day when people celebrate a person or event
7. birthday	•	•	make something look attractive
8. celebrate	•	•	do something special, such as have a party

C. Choose the correct word from the box to complete the sentences.

1. Independence Day is the writer's favorite _____.

2. His school organizes a big _____ to celebrate the nation's independence.

3. They _____ the yard with colorful banners and balloons.

4. They place small _____ on the table to honor the nation.

5. My _____ is on Tuesday. I will be 14 years old!

Simple Present of the verb *Be* in Yes / No Questions

The **simple present** tense of the verb **be** is often used in questions with the answer *yes* or *no*. In the simple present, the verb *be* describes a general or present state.

Example: *Is* your birthday in June?   *Yes, it is. / No, it isn't.*

A. Look at the picture and ask Yes / No questions using the verb *be*.

B. Complete the conversation using the correct present tense form of the verb *be*.

Julie: Hi, Kyra, this is a great party! Is this your sister?

Kyra: No, she isn't. Ling (1) __is__ my cousin. She speaks French, English, and Chinese.

Julie: (2) __Are__ you from Canada, Ling?

Ling: Yes, I (3) __am__ from Vancouver. There (4) __are__ many nationalities in Vancouver.

Julie: (5) __Are__ you an immigrant?

Ling: No, I was born in Vancouver. My dad (6) __is__ Canadian, and my mom is from Hong Kong.

C. Circle the correct words to complete the questions.

1. (**Is** / Are) your birthday in January?

2. (Is / **Are**) the invitations ready?

3. (**Is** / Are) she from this neighborhood?

4. (**Is** / Are) your sister 15 years old?

Count and Noncount Nouns

A **count noun** is something that can be counted. The plural of a count noun usually ends in *-s* or *-es*. A **noncount noun** is something that you can't cut into parts and count. Noncount nouns usually do not have a plural form.

Examples:
Count nouns include *book, child, flag,* and *balloon*.
Noncount nouns include *bread, water, money, humor, weather, education,* and *furniture*.

some / any / a / an	Example sentences
Use *some* with count nouns and noncount nouns.	Mexicans take *some flowers* to the cemetery. They place *some food* on the altar.
Use *any* for questions and negative sentences with count nouns and noncount nouns.	Are there *any apples* left for the cake? We don't have *any milk* or *any cookies*. Is there *any money* to buy more decorations?
Use *a / an* for singular count nouns.	They also make *an* offering or *a* house altar.

For grammar reference, go to Grammar Appendix.

I want *some* water and cookies.

Is there *any* more pizza?

That's *a* birthday cake.

D. Choose the correct answer.

1. Are there any _____ on the table?

   a. flower   b. flowers   c. a flower

2. There is _____ water in the glass.

   a. a   b. any   c. some

3. Is there _____ candle on the altar?

   a. a   b. any   c. some

4. I can see _____ people at the party.

   a. a   b. any   c. some

5. I can't see _____ children at the party.

   a. a   b. any   c. some

6. Is there _____ cake left on the table?

   a. a   b. any   c. some

E. Check (✓) the sentences that are correct. Rewrite the incorrect ones.

☑ 1. I am reading a book.

_____

☑ 2. John is buying some socks.

_____ John is buing some socks

☒ 3. There aren't some trees in the park.

_____ There is not some trees in the park

☑ 4. Do you have any chairs for them?

_____

☑ 5. We don't have some milk in the kitchen.

_____

Pair and Share

With a partner, ask and answer these questions.

Is he your friend?

Yes . . .

Are there any _____ in the kitchen?

Yes, there are some . . .

**Listening Strategy:
Identify main ideas**

Identifying the main ideas helps you understand what people say.

What are people mostly talking about?

That is the main idea.

Before Listening

A. Look at the pictures. How old are the young people? Where are they from?

B. Listen to the audio. Match the pictures with the names. Write the numbers.

_____ Maria, Puerto Rico   _____ Kelly, United States   _____ Lev, United States   _____ Huan, China

After Listening

C. Turn to another student in your class. Say your name and where you are from. Tell what your favorite celebration is and why.

5 | **Pronunciation**

Intonation in Yes / No Questions

Intonation rises on the last word of a yes / no question.

A. Listen. Write *falling intonation* or *rising intonation* for the last word.

1. Where is the party?   _____

2. Is it far from your home?   _____

3. Did you buy a gift?   _____

4. What did you buy?   _____

5. Are many people invited?   _____

6. May I see the invitation?   _____

B. Listen to the audio and repeat.

**Speaking Strategy:
Decline an invitation**

If you cannot attend a celebration or a party, say that you are sorry and give a reason why you cannot attend. Always thank the person for inviting you.

• I'm sorry, I can't.
• I have a lot of homework.
• Maybe next time.
• Thank you for the invitation.

 A. Listen to the conversations and complete the sentences. Listen again and check your answers.

Conversation 1	Conversation 2
Lucy: Can you come over on my sister's birthday? We're having a barbecue.	**Ling:** Kim, I'm having a Halloween party on Saturday. Do you want to come?
Tim: Sounds good. When is it?	**Kim:** Oh, on Saturday? (1) _____. My sister is having a party, too.
Lucy: This Saturday.	**Ling:** Oh, that's too bad.
Tim: I'd love to, but I can't. (1) _____ this weekend.	**Kim:** But (2) _____.
Lucy: That's too bad.	**Ling:** Well, have a good time at your sister's party.
Tim: (2) _____.	

B. Your Turn

Roleplay the conversations with a partner. What would Kim say at the end of the conversation? Write your answer.

Your idea: _____

_____

Pair and Share

Invite your partner to a party. He/She must politely refuse and say why. Switch roles.

I'm having a birthday party next Saturday. Can you come?

I'm sorry . . .

 C. Listen to the audio. Take notes to prepare for a conversation about party invitations.

**Reading Strategy:
Read for the main idea**

The main idea is the most important idea in a text.

• Find what is most important.
• Look for specific details.

Before Reading

A. Look at these pictures. What do Malaysian people celebrate?

B. Read the text. Underline specific details to help you find the main idea.

🔊 Malaysia: Land of Many

Malaysia is a Southeast Asian country that has a lot of variety. The word *malay* indicates "many," and Malaysia certainly is a varied country. Most Malaysians come from Malaysia, China, and India. The country's main religions are Islam, Buddhism, and Christianity. The Malaysians speak Bahasa Malaysia, English, Chinese, and many more languages.

Because of its unique mixture, Malaysia has a lot of different **holidays** and **festivals**. *Diwali* or *deepavali* is the "festival of lights." This ancient Hindu festival is **celebrated** in autumn every year. Hindus clean their houses and **decorate** them with lanterns and lights. They eat good food and go shopping.

The Chinese in Malaysia celebrate Chinese **New Year** in January or February. They often **organize** an "open house," where friends and family can come and visit—no matter their race or religion. When preparing for the New Year, people say only positive comments and try to be nice to everybody!

Hari Raya means "Celebration Day" in Arabic. *Hari Raya Aidilfitri* is a Muslim festival celebrated at the end of Ramadan. During the month of Ramadan, Muslims don't eat or drink from sunrise to sunset. So, at the end of Ramadan, they celebrate *Hari Raya Aidilfitri* with prayer, food, and general happiness. They decorate their houses with green, yellow, and gold lights. They visit their family and friends' houses. The festival can last an entire month, but only the first two days are public holidays in Malaysia.

After Reading

C. Complete the chart with details from the text.

Festival	Time of Year	Religious / Ethnic Group
		Hindu
	January / February	
Hari Raya Aidilfitri		

D. Write the main idea of the article.

_____

_____

8 | Writing ✏️

A. With your partner, choose a sentence and add a detail to it.

1. The party was at a house.

2. There were decorations.

3. We ate food.

B. Add details to this paragraph. Use the Internet to find more information.

People celebrate Chinese New Year. People get together. When preparing for the New Year, people are nice. Fireworks are popular, too. For the Lantern Festival, people make lanterns. They eat soup with dumplings. The celebration lasts for days. People are happy.

Details to Add

• Who celebrates Chinese New Year? Where?

• When is Chinese New Year?

• How are people nice? What do they do?

• Where do the fireworks happen?

• Who celebrates the Lantern Festival?

• When is the Lantern Festival?

• How many days does the celebration last?

Writing Strategy:
Add specific details

Add details to your main ideas to make your writing more interesting. Tell *who, what, when, where, which, why,* and *how.* For example:

• Where does the action happen?

• Why does it happen?

• Who is there?

• What do people do?

• What other details could you add?

UNIT 3   **Daily Lives**

In this unit, I will learn to . . .

- ask and answer questions about daily routines.
- talk about how often something happens.
- listen and read for specific time phrases.

1 | Get Ready

  What is a day in your life like?

 A. Look at the pictures and read the descriptions.

Where Dmitri lives, the schools don't teach English. He learns English at home every day. His father **normally** teaches him an hour every day.

Lee lives in Alaska, and his school is very far away. So, Lee **always** studies with his father at home in the morning. He plays with his friends in the afternoons.

Frank is sick, and he doesn't have the energy to go to school. A tutor comes to his house twice a week.

Lanfen is 15, and she goes to university. She is **usually** the youngest person in a class, but she's very happy. She's studying geography.

B. Answer the questions. Then listen to Lina's experiences and check your answers.

1. Do homeschooled kids have a lot of free time?

   _____

2. Do homeschoolers have many friends?

   _____

3. Can homeschoolers have a tutor?

   _____

4. Can homeschoolers go to university?

   _____

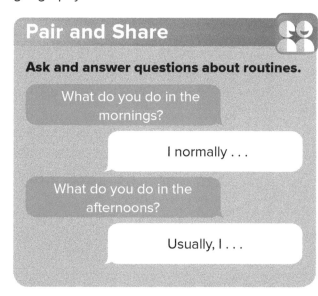

Pair and Share

Ask and answer questions about routines.

> What do you do in the mornings?

> I normally . . .

> What do you do in the afternoons?

> Usually, I . . .

A. Listen to the audio and read along. Guess the meaning of the words in bold.

I am **always** busy. During the week, I **go** to school to learn about science, literature, math, and history. After school, I work at a store. I **arrive** home and help my parents **make dinner**. My father is a great cook, so **sometimes**, I **take a selfie** in front of the food to show my friends how good our meals are! After homework, I **usually** watch a TV show or read. On weekends, I **clean up** my room and go to the store to work for a few hours. Then **normally** I play baseball with my friends and do more homework. It's a busy life!

Word Box

always
arrive
clean up
go
make
make dinner
never
normally
sometimes
take
take a selfie/
  a picture
usually

B. Match the correct actions to the pictures above.

1. ___ take a selfie   3. ___ do nothing   5. ___ clean up your room

2. ___ arrive home   4. ___ go to school   6. ___ make dinner

C. Match the words that go together. There are two correct answers for every verb.

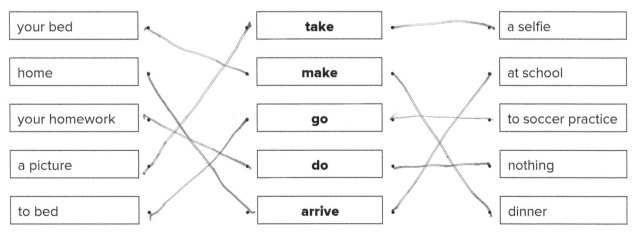

your bed		**take**		a selfie
home		**make**		at school
your homework		**go**		to soccer practice
a picture		**do**		nothing
to bed		**arrive**		dinner

Questions with *How often*

Questions that begin with the words *How often* are answered with time words such as *usually, normally, twice a week, once a month, never,* or *always.*

Examples:

How often do you organize your bedroom?
I organize my room *every day / once a week / twice a month / three times a year.*

A. Write three questions that begin with *How often*. Then answer them.

1. Question: How often _____?

   Answer: _____.

2. Question: How often _____?

   Answer: _____.

3. Question: How often _____?

   Answer: _____.

She *always* plays the guitar.

He *normally* walks his dog in the morning.

Adverbs of Frequency

Adverbs tell something about the verb. An **adverb of frequency** is used to tell how often something happens. The following are adverbs of frequency: *always, frequently, never, normally, often, sometimes,* and *usually.*

Frequency	Example sentences
★ ★ ★ ★ ★	I *always* make my bed.
★ ★ ★ ★	My mom *usually / normally* makes a sandwich for me.
★ ★	We *sometimes* make dinner together.
	My brother *never* cleans the bathroom.

For grammar reference, go to Grammar Appendix.

B. Underline examples of adverbs of frequency in the text.

Hello, my name is Paula, and I have a problem. My parents are very strict! They always check if my room is clean. I can never arrive home after 8 p.m. My mother usually prepares peanut butter sandwiches for lunch because peanut butter is healthy, but I don't like peanut butter! I've told her many times, but she never listens to me. My father sometimes plays basketball with me, but only after I finish my homework. When I'm a parent, my children are going to clean their rooms when they want. They are going to eat what they want for lunch. They are going to play sports before finishing their homework!

C. Complete the text with the words from the box.

A:	Hey, Duane. You look upset. What's up?
B:	My parents want me to help them all the time. I make breakfast every morning. Also, every (1) _____, I prepare my lunch for school. Three (2) _____ a week, I help clean the house. I don't make my bed, but I clean up my room once (3) _____ week.
A:	It's not so bad. But do they let you play soccer?
B:	Well, yes. My mom normally takes me to soccer practice, but she (4) _____ picks me up. I always have to take the bus home. Oh, and I take my little brother to school (5) _____ morning. Is it normal to do so many things all the time?
A:	Yes, Duane, it is normal to be busy.

times   morning   never
always   every   a

Know how to vs *Learn how to*

Knowing and *learning* are different. **Know how to** means to have the ability to do something. **Learn how to** means beginning to understand something through study or practice.

Examples:

I *know how to* play the piano. I play it every day.

I don't know how to play the piano. I want to *learn how to* play it.

D. Complete the sentences using *know how to* or *learn how to.*

1. Joe has taken art classes for many years. He _____ use oil and watercolors.

2. Nina has helped make dinner since she was little. She _____ be safe in the kitchen.

3. Jose is taking classes in fencing. He wants to _____ fence.

4. Amanda wants to _____ swim. She hopes to be a good swimmer by next year.

5. Peter received a new camera two years ago; now he _____ take perfect pictures.

Pair and Share

With a partner, ask and answer questions about your routines.

What do you normally do on the weekend?

I normally . . .

How often do you help make dinner?

I make dinner . . .

Listening Strategy:
Listen for time words and phrases

Listening for words and phrases that express time helps you identify when and how often things happen. Focus on words such as *always, never, sometimes, usually,* and *normally*.

Before Listening

A. Look at the pictures. How important is music to these people? How important is music to you?

B. Listen to the audio. Complete the chart. Listen again to check your answers.

For _____	music is _____	because _____.
Olivia	very important	she plays the drums.
Leah	important	
Mac		
Sue		
Lara		she goes dancing every Saturday.

After Listening

C. What is something you always do? Sometimes do? Never do? Share with a partner.

5 | Pronunciation

Sentence Stress with Adverbs of Frequency

In sentences with adverbs of frequency, stress the adverb of frequency for added importance.

A. Listen. Circle the frequency adverbs if they are stressed.

1. always
2. normally
3. normally
4. usually
5. always
6. usually

B. Listen to the audio and repeat. Stress the words that are stressed.

**Speaking Strategy:
Expressions that tell "*how often*"**

Use time words and phrases to describe how often you do an activity.

- She *usually* copies the sentences.
- He reads a comic book *twice a week*.
- *How often* do you visit your grandparents?

A. Listen to the conversation and complete the sentences. Listen and check your answers.

Beatrice: What (1) _____ your day look like?

Dmitri: Well, my sister and I (2) _____ go to school in the morning. We (3) _____ arrive home at 2 o'clock.

Beatrice: Do you have your English classes then?

Dmitri: No, we are (4) _____ hungry. We always have lunch first.

Beatrice: Of course. And then?

Dmitri: Our mom almost always teaches us English. We (5) _____ use a book, but other times we watch a movie on the Internet. We like to learn online.

Beatrice: Do you sing songs, too?

Dmitri: No! My sister sings really well, but I sing terribly badly! I like to do art.

B. Your Turn

Roleplay the conversation with a partner. What other question would Beatrice ask? Write your answer.

Your idea: _____

_____

Pair and Share

With a partner, choose a person from the Get Ready page and have a similar conversation.

 C. Listen to the audio. Take notes to prepare for a conversation about someone's daily routine.

Before Reading

A. Look at the pictures. How many Olympic sports can you name? How do you become an Olympic athlete?

Reading Strategy:
Read for specific time phrases

As you read, look for words and phrases that tell you how often things happen.

- Words such as *normally, never, usually,* and *always* give information about a person's habits and schedule.
- Time phrases can help you put events in order.

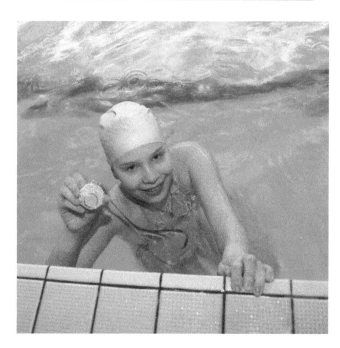

B. Read the text. Circle the time words and phrases.

 An interview with Olympic Swimmers

Ryan and Paola are swimmers on the United Kingdom Olympic team. What does the life of an athlete in training look like?

Paola: Kids on the Olympic team **normally** train for 4 to 8 years. We need to train a lot: 3 times a day, 6 days a week.

Ryan: We **always** wake up at 4:30 and run for an hour. Then we **go** to the pool and swim 4,000 meters. We have breakfast, and we **usually take** a shower before going to school. **Sometimes** there's no time for a shower. We have school just like other kids.

Paola: Yes, but during school, we always have strength training for an hour or two. Then we normally have lunch. We always eat a lot: twice the calories that our friends eat.

Ryan: In the afternoon, we go to the pool and swim for 3 hours. Then we go home and eat dinner. Paola, how often do your parents let you sleep late on weekends?

Paola: **Never**! I know that I need to train hard every day to swim in the Olympics.

Ryan: When you want to **make** it to the Olympic team, you need to train more than you want, eat more than you can, get up earlier, go to bed earlier, and sleep more than 8 hours.

After Reading

C. Number the events in the correct order from 1 to 10.

_7_ eat lunch   _4_ take a shower   _5_ go to school

_10_ go to bed   _3_ eat breakfast   _9_ eat dinner

_1_ wake up   _2_ swim 4 kilometers

_8_ swim 3 hours   _6_ do strength training

D. Make a chart with three columns. List items from your routine and daily life. Compare your chart with a partner.

Things you always do	Things you usually do	Things you never do

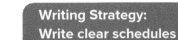

8 | **Writing**

Writing Strategy:
Write clear schedules

Writing a monthly schedule helps people plan their activities. A monthly schedule includes:

• regular activities, such as sports events, family activities.
• special occasions, such as birthdays or holidays.
• obligations, such as a doctor appointment.
• school activities, such as homework.

A. Tell your partner about your activities for this week.

Question: How often do you (go to your math class)?

Answer: Five times a week. Monday through Friday.

B. Complete a monthly calendar of your activities. Follow the example.

October						
Sun	Mon	Tue	Wed	Thu	Fri	Sat
3 Visit my grandparents	4	5 Guitar class	6 Luke's birthday	7 Volleyball practice	8	9 Volleyball match
10 Study for the math test!	11	12 Math test Guitar class	13	14 Volleyball practice	15	16 Volleyball match Mom's birthday

C. Write two sentences about your activities for a week.

ABC **Vocabulary**

A. Write sentences using words from the box.

always	normally	sometimes	almost never	never

1. (Mother's Day) *On Mother's Day, my family normally has dinner in a nice restaurant.*

2. (New Year's Day) We eat dinner at home and always do a party

3. (Christmas) We open we present and eat dinner.

4. (Independence Day) _____

5. (birthday) We go eat in a restaurent.

6. (holiday) _____

B. Label the pictures.

1.
_____

3.
_____

2.
_____

4.
_____

C. Circle the correct words.

1. Isabel will (make / organize / take) the party for all the neighbors.

2. My aunt and I look alike; we have the (different / same / warm) dark hair.

3. DeMarco (gathers / makes / takes) toys from wood.

4. Dan and I like (clean / different / same) kinds of movies. He likes action movies, but I like comedies.

5. Akara will (celebrate / go / take) to university next year.

Grammar

A. Circle the correct words.

1. Martin usually doesn't (go / goes) out so late.

2. (Do you / You do) often work out on the weekends?

3. Paola (knows / learns) how to swim really well.

4. (Are / Is) there any furniture in the apartment?

5. (Is / Are) Bill and Peter brothers or cousins?

6. Carla wants (to learn / learning) how to draw a comic.

B. Complete each sentence using words from the box.

How	When	Where	Why	Who

1. _Who_ is your math teacher?   *Mr. Lee teaches us math.*

2. _When_ do you study Japanese?   *I study Japanese on Tuesday nights.*

3. _Why_ do you go to Hawaii every summer?   *We go to visit our relatives there.*

4. _How_ do you celebrate the New Year?   *We have a party with family and friends.*

5. _When_ is the party?   *It is at Kevin's place.*

C. Complete each sentence using *some, any, a,* or *an.*

1. We don't have _any_ rice.

2. Grandma wants _some_ tea.

3. Put _some_ soy sauce in the soup.

4. There aren't _any_ more presents under the Christmas tree.

5. I send her _an_ invitation to the Chinese New Year's celebration every year.

6. We make a scary face on _a_ pumpkin on Halloween.

D. Complete these sentences about yourself.

1. I want to _speack english_ .

2. I don't have any _phones_ .

3. I want some _cake_ .

4. I always _like the switch_ .

5. I never _do my homwork_ .

6. I _eat my breakfast_ every day.

  Reading: Social Studies

Cultural Differences around the World

Today we are more similar than ever before. English has become the global language. People in **different** countries wear similar clothes, watch similar movies, and have similar interests. However, we are also still different. The biggest differences are our cultural traditions.

Do you live in a town or city, or do you live in the countryside? Do you live in a house or in an apartment? Of the 7 billion people in the world, more than half live in cities and towns. Life in the countryside is **normally** slower than in the big cities, and the way of life affects people's personalities.

Every country and many areas within a country have their typical dishes, and some food is **prepared** for special celebrations. At parties and **festivals**, we dance or play special music. Do you know a dance from your region or your country?

Different cultures have different ways of showing love and affection. For example, in Latin America, it is common for a teenage girl to greet a classmate (boy or girl) with a kiss on the cheek. In Northern Europe, this would not be acceptable. In Germany, men and women shake hands, but boys and girls rarely touch each other to say hello. How do you greet your classmates—more like in Latin America or more like Germany?

Cultures are also unique in their music, films, and sports. Some of these are global. For example, Hollywood action films are watched throughout the world. But others are more local. Masala films from India have a mixture of action, comedy, romance, and drama. Masala films are not very popular outside of India.

A. Read the sentences and circle T for *True* or F for *False*.

1. People around the world are becoming more different.　　(T)　　F

2. People who live in cities and people who live in the countryside have different lifestyles.　　(T)　　F

3. Celebrations show a variety of cultural traditions.　　(T)　　F

4. In Germany, students kiss their classmates.　　T　　(F)

5. Masala films are enjoyed around the world.　　T　　(F)

B. Answer the four questions in the text.

1. Do you live in a town or city, or do you live in the countryside?

   I live in a city

2. Do you live in a house or in an apartment?

   Im a house

3. Do you know a dance from your region or your country?

   No, I ~~All~~ don't.

4. How do you greet your classmates—more like in Latin America or more like Germany?

   I don't no

C. With a classmate, make a Venn diagram to show how you and your classmate are similar and how you are different.

Project

In this project, describe your dream home, write about your daily routine, and give a presentation about your dream home. Use what you know from Units 1 to 3 to complete the project.

How are we alike and different?

Step 1   Brainstorm

What is your dream home like?

Location	Rooms	Style

Step 2   Plan

What is your typical daily routine in your dream home?

In the morning, I _____. Then, I _____

_____. After that, I _____

_____ . I also

_____

_____

_____ .

Step 3   Prepare

Prepare a one-minute presentation to describe your dream home to your partner.

Use these questions to help you prepare:

1. What rooms are in your dream home?
2. Where is your dream home?
3. What do you do in your dream home?
4. Why do you like your dream home?
5. What is special about your dream home?

Step 4   Record

Write the similarities and differences between your classmate's dream home and your dream home.

Creative Zone

Start a new celebration

A. Choose a reason to celebrate.

important person

a tradition

important event

B. Choose something to do.

fireworks

a parade

music

C. Give your celebration a name. _The Masc'es Day_

D. Explain your celebration to a partner. Use the phrases below.	
1. My celebration is called . . . (name) *Masc'esday*	5. On this day, everyone wears in (describe clothes) *black*
2. We celebrate *Me* (reason)	6. People also like to eat *Very* (food)
3. We celebrate it on the 5th day of every *April* (name of month)	7. I like this day because . *It's my day !!!*
4. People like to *Sing* (action)	

E. Use these prompts to ask questions about your partner's celebration.	
1. What / called?	3. When / celebrate?
2. Why / have / celebration?	4. What / people / do?

4 | Time

5 | Now and Then

6 | Giving Advice

How does the past shape us?

 Look at the picture. Read the unit topics and answer the questions.

- **What in the picture is new? What is old?**

- **What do you see in your life that is old? What is new?**

- **How is your life similar to your parents' lives when they were your age?**

CAN DO statements

After the next three units, you will be able to . . .

• talk about the people in your family.

• talk about the past and the present.

• say how time influences your life.

In this unit, I will learn to . . .
• say how time influences my life.
• use the simple past.
• identify cause and effect and give reasons.

1 | Get Ready

 How important is time to you?

A. Look at the pictures and read the captions. What kinds of changes do you think these people made? Listen to the audio to find out.

Mr. Benson never had any money when he was young. Now he's learned his lesson.

Mr. Jones ate a lot of junk food when he was younger. Now he has a healthy lifestyle.

Mrs. Park used to work a lot. Her family is more important to her now.

B. In pairs, talk about an adult in your family. What is he or she like? How did he or she change over time?

C. Read and circle **T** for *True* or **F** for *False*. Correct the false statements.

My grandmother lives with us in our **apartment**. When she was young, she owned a restaurant, so she knows a lot about cooking. She doesn't work anymore, so she has lots of time to cook at home. Sometimes she asks me to help, and I **do my best**. I know it **makes her happy**. She teaches me a lot of her "secrets" and other **stuff**. Maybe one day I'll be a chef, too.

1. Her grandmother works in a restaurant.   T (F)

_____

2. Her grandmother doesn't like cooking, (T) F
   but she does it anyway.

_____

3. Her grandmother doesn't share her   T (F)
   cooking secrets.

_____

Pair and Share

Ask and answer about different times in your life.

> What did you like to do when you were younger? How are you different today?

> When I was a kid, I liked to play with my toys at home. Now I like to play outside.

Ask and answer questions about grown-ups in your family.

> Do you have a favorite aunt, uncle, or grandparent? What are they like?

> My grandmother is lots of fun. She . . .

A. Listen to the audio and read along. Guess the meaning of the words in bold.

Hi, I'm Ben Carlson, and I have a son and a **daughter**, Derek and Michelle. They are **teenagers**. We live in an **apartment**. Michelle finished high school three months **ago**. **Last** month, Michelle got a **job** at a store. It was her first job, and she was nervous. She said, "I can't wear **sneakers** to work, and I have to wear my uniform. I can't arrive to work **late**. I need to **do my best**." **Yesterday**, Michelle's friends went to visit her at the store. They said nice **stuff** about her, like, "You look very good in your uniform." That **made her happy**.

Word Box

ago
apartment
daughter
do your best
job
last
late
make someone
   happy
sneakers
stuff
teenager
yesterday

A   B   C

B. Look at the pictures. Number them in order.

1. _____   2. _____   3. _____.

C. Choose the correct word from the box to complete the sentences. Then listen to check your answers.

1. Mr. Carlson has a son and a _____.

2. She isn't a little girl; she's a _____.

3. They live in an _____.

4. Michelle finished high school three months _____.

5. Last month, Michelle got a _____ at a store.

6. Michelle said, "I can't wear _____ to work."

7. "I can't arrive to work _____."

8. "I need to _____ my best."

9. Yesterday, Michelle's friends told her, "You look very good in your uniform." That made her _____.

Regular and Irregular Verbs in the Simple Past

Verbs in the **simple past** can be **regular** (ending in -*ed*) or **irregular** (for example, *write → wrote*). Memorize the irregular forms.

Questions with Regular and Irregular Verbs in the Simple Past

Simple past, *to be*	Examples
Yes / No question	Grandpa, **was** money important to you?
Answer	No. When I **was** a young man, money **wasn't** important to me.

Simple past, action verbs	Examples
Wh- question	What **did** you **learn**?
Answer	I **learned** that I **didn't need** any gadgets.

For grammar reference, go to Grammar Appendix.

A. Match the verbs to their past tense forms. Then circle R for *Regular* or for *Irregular*.

1. read	studied (R / I)
2. study	was, were (R / I)
3. drink	read (R / I)
4. be	danced (R / I)
5. dance	drank (R / I)

B. Look at the pictures and read the text below. Underline examples of irregular verbs in the text.

The History of Credit Cards

At the beginning of the 20th century, a few large stores gave credit cards to their clients. The cards were only good at those stores. Then, in 1946, Brooklyn banker John Biggins introduced a card called Charg-It. The card was only for customers with an account at the Biggins Bank, but they could use it at different stores.

C. Choose the correct answers.

1. About 100 years ago, some people _____ a credit card at a large store.

   a. can get
   b. could get
   c. didn't get

2. John Biggins _____ a credit card that people could use at different stores.

   a. invents
   b. invented
   c. inventing

3. Customers _____ their Charg-It card just like cash.

   a. used
   b. didn't use
   c. will use

4. Charg-It cards _____ only for customers with accounts at the Biggins Bank.

   a. were
   b. is
   c. was

D. Complete the sentences with the correct form of the verb.

1. McNamara _invented_ (invent) the credit card at a restaurant.

2. McNamara had the idea when he _forgot_ (forget) his money one day.

3. Credit cards _____ (be) not always plastic.

4. By 1965, there _____ (be) 1,000,000 credit cards.

Intensifiers

Intensifiers give emphasis to verbs, adjectives, and adverbs. For example, in *I am very tired,* the intensifier *very* tells us how tired the person is. Other examples of intensifiers are:

He studies *quite* hard.

He *really* wants to succeed.

He gets *extremely* high marks.

E. Circle the intensifiers in the text.

I really like listening to music, but I don't know how to play a musical instrument. I really want to learn how to play the guitar. My cousin can play the guitar incredibly fast, and he sings quite nicely too. I can't sing very well. I don't know if I can learn; I'm extremely impatient!

Pair and Share

Talk to a partner about credit cards.

Do you think credit cards are good or bad?

They're good to have, but you should be very careful with them.

Do you think teenagers should have credit cards? Why or why not?

I think . . .

**Listening Strategy:
Predict from pictures**

Predicting from pictures helps you prepare for a listening.

Before Listening

A. Look at the pictures below. How do these people use their time?

 B. Listen to the TV show. Then write the letters of the expressions next to the pictures.

a. She can save his life, but she's **pressed for time**.

b. Why doesn't she talk to me? She's **wasting her time** with the phone.

c. We'll do our homework later, Mom. **All in good time**.

d. **At this point in time** my mom's company is doing very well.

After Listening

C. In pairs, discuss this question. How do you spend your time on the weekend?

 5 | **Pronunciation**

Informal speaking: Don't and Didn't

Sometimes when you speak, you say the words quickly so that the end of one word blends with the beginning of the next word. This is a form of informal speaking. When you say the words *don't* and *didn't*, the final -*t* is often silent.

 A. Listen and read the following sentences. Draw a line to show the words that are blended together.

1. We don't have time.

2. We don't need all that stuff.

3. He didn't wear sneakers to school.

4. We didn't go.

5. She didn't pay in cash.

6. I don't like the apartment.

 B. Listen and repeat.

Conversation

Speaking Strategy:
Indicate time

When you speak, use time words to let your listeners know when events happen.

 A. Listen to the conversation and complete the sentences. Then listen again and check your answers.

Diane: How was your weekend?

Ron: Great! I went to the North Mall (1) _____ Saturday afternoon.

Diane: Really? We went (2) _____ Friday. (3) _____ my sister wanted to buy a new pair of sneakers, but (4) _____ we had to hurry. We were pressed for time because the movie started (5) _____ 5 p.m.

Ron: My friends and I went to the movies, too. Did you see *Cash or Credit*? It was so funny!

Diane: No, we saw *10,000 Years Ago*. It was such a boring movie! I think I'll see *Cash or Credit* (6) _____ time.

Ron: You'd better go (7) _____. We had to see the (8) _____ show because it was sold out.

B. Your Turn

Roleplay the conversation with a partner. How would Diane respond? Write your answer in the blank space.

Your idea: _____

_____

 C. Listen to the audio and take notes. Prepare to ask and answer questions about last weekend.

Pair and Share

With a partner, ask and answer questions about last weekend.

 Hey, Robin! How was your weekend?

It was . . .

Reading

Before Reading

A. Look at the pictures. What do you think the main idea of the text will be?

> **Reading Strategy:**
> **Read for causes and effects**
>
> Some texts explain the cause of, or reason for, an action. Read to find the reason for an action.
>
> • First, read the article for the main idea.
> • Then read again, looking for causes and effects. Ask, *Why did this happen?*
> • Give reasons using sentences that start with *Because . . .*

B. Read the text and underline causes and effects.

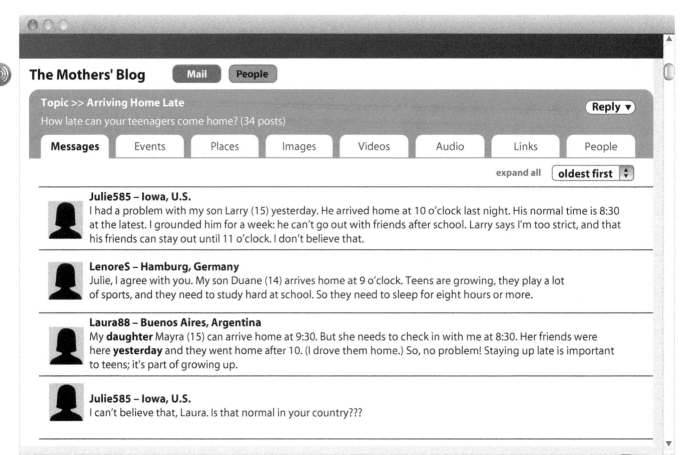

The Mothers' Blog [Mail] [People]

Topic >> Arriving Home Late [Reply ▾]
How late can your teenagers come home? (34 posts)

| **Messages** | Events | Places | Images | Videos | Audio | Links | People |

expand all [oldest first ⬍]

Julie585 – Iowa, U.S.
I had a problem with my son Larry (15) yesterday. He arrived home at 10 o'clock last night. His normal time is 8:30 at the latest. I grounded him for a week: he can't go out with friends after school. Larry says I'm too strict, and that his friends can stay out until 11 o'clock. I don't believe that.

LenoreS – Hamburg, Germany
Julie, I agree with you. My son Duane (14) arrives home at 9 o'clock. Teens are growing, they play a lot of sports, and they need to study hard at school. So they need to sleep for eight hours or more.

Laura88 – Buenos Aires, Argentina
My **daughter** Mayra (15) can arrive home at 9:30. But she needs to check in with me at 8:30. Her friends were here **yesterday** and they went home after 10. (I drove them home.) So, no problem! Staying up late is important to teens; it's part of growing up.

Julie585 – Iowa, U.S.
I can't believe that, Laura. Is that normal in your country???

After Reading

C. Answer the questions.

1. Why did Larry's mom ground him for a week?

_____

2. Why does Duane's mom agree with Larry's mother?

_____

3. Does Mayra's mother agree with the other mothers? Why or why not?

_____

D. Complete the chart to show different causes and effects.

Cause	Effect
You stayed out too late with friends.	
	You got a bad grade on the test.
	Your mom took away your phone.

8 | Writing

Writing Strategy: Use time expressions

- You can use time expressions such as *yesterday, last week, two days ago,* at the beginning or at the end of a sentence.
- If a phrase is at the beginning of a sentence, use a comma. Don't use a comma if it's at the end of the sentence.

A. In pairs, circle all the time expressions in the text.

Don't Have Money? Barter!

Last March, we visited the Annual Caleno Bartering Convention and interviewed Mrs. Lewis, a visitor, on March 27.

Mrs. Lewis: "I have a large house, and I'm making a new garden. The tools and plants can be expensive, so I placed an advertisement on the Internet last week. I received three good offers for plants and one for tools. At this moment I'm looking for a wooden fence."

Caleno Times: "What products or services did you offer in exchange?"

Mrs. Lewis: "I am a school teacher. I helped two teenagers prepare for exams last month. Helping students is an excellent barter."

B. Rewrite the sentences and add time expressions.

1. She eats a sandwich.

2. I was sad, but my brother cheered me up.

3. Where did you go?

4. She bought new sneakers.

5. We have a test.

6. We have PE class.

7. My mom got a new job.

C. Write a paragraph about what you did last weekend using time expressions.

In this unit, I will learn to . . .
• talk about the past and the present.
• use indefinite pronouns: *someone, nothing,* . . .
• listen and put events in order.

1 | Get Ready

Do you think change is good? Why or why not?

A. Look at the pictures and discuss. Do you wish that you grew up in the 1990s? How do you feel technology has changed us? Listen to the audio.

Nobody had a cell phone in 1990. If you got lost, you had to go to a pay phone. More often than not, plans were made in advance. If you wanted to **meet** your friends at the **mall**, it was **impossible** to change the **meeting point** at the last minute.

Social media didn't **exist**. There was only one phone at home, and someone was always using it. On the other hand, teens met in person all the time. They had many parties and **get-togethers**.

It was harder to find information. Today, you can **quickly** look up information for your homework on the Internet. In 1990, teenagers spent a lot more time doing **research** at the library. They relied on books and articles. It took a lot longer than it does today. Aren't you glad you live in the present?

B. Match the words to their meaning.

1. mall	come together to talk
2. meet	in a short time
3. (didn't) exist	a place with many stores
4. impossible	not possible
5. get-together	there weren't any
6. quickly	investigation
7. research	an informal social meeting
8. meeting point	a specific place where you meet others

Pair and Share

With a partner, ask and answer questions about the past and present.

> What's another thing that's changing?

> People don't buy CDs and DVDs anymore. Everything is online.

Ask and answer questions about these changes.

> Do you think these changes are good or bad?

> In some ways, it's good . . .

A. Listen to the audio and read along. Guess the meaning of the words in bold.

WOMAN: You go to the local **market** a lot. Why?

MAN: I like the markets. The people are nice and the food is **cheap**. You can **quickly** buy what you need. A market is a good **meeting point** for **get-togethers**. What do you think?

WOMAN: Hmm, I actually like the **mall**. You can find so many stores there. It's **impossible** to find good clothes in a market. And it's easier for me to **meet** my friends there!

MAN: That's true. Markets have **existed** for a long time, and they are good for some things. But times are **changing**: there are more malls and fewer markets. It's not a **problem**, really. You just need to go to the market for some things and the mall for other things.

WOMAN: Hmm, maybe you're right! I guess I should **research** where I can get what I want.

Word Box

change
cheap
exist
get-together
impossible
mall
market
meet
meeting point
problem
quickly
research

B. Match the phrases to the pictures.

1. _____ walking in the mall

2. _____ a meeting point

3. _____ vegetables in a market

4. _____ doing research in the library

5. _____ cheap food

6. _____ passing the ball quickly

C. Complete the sentences using the correct words from the box. Then listen and check your answers.

The man says a market is a good (1) _____ for get-togethers and the food is
(2) _____. The woman thinks it is (3) _____ to buy good clothes at the market and
she prefers to go to the (4) _____. The man says that the times are (5) _____ and
that markets are disappearing.

There was / There were

Use **there was** and **there were** to describe existence in the past.

A. In pairs, look at the pictures and discuss the differences between them. Use *there was / there were* and *there is / there are* when possible.

B. Complete the conversations with the correct forms from the box.

there was	there were	was there
there wasn't	there weren't	were there

1.

Ryan: How was the party last Saturday?

Seth: It was really good.

Ryan: _____ a lot of people?

Seth: Yes, _____ .

2.

Ryan: _____ good food?

Seth: Yes! _____ hamburgers and salads. _____ any sodas, but _____ fresh fruit drinks.

3.

Ryan: _____ a DJ?

Seth: No, _____ .
But _____ good music. Everybody danced. I'm sorry you couldn't go to the party.

Ryan: Yeah, me too. Maybe next time.

C. Choose the correct answers.

1. Before the year 1900, _____ only one style for young boys and girls: long white dresses.

   a. there are   b. there was   c. is there

2. Before 1900, _____ any children's clothes in the U.S. Kids wore small adults' clothes.

   a. wasn't there   b. there aren't   c. there weren't

3. In the 19th century, _____ any difference in colors for boys' and girls' clothes.

    a. there wasn't   b. was there   c. there weren't

4. A: _____ do boys wear blue and girls pink?

   B: Because after 1900, boys and girls were dressed differently.

    a. Why   b. How   c. What time

5. A: Why did children have two sets of clothes?

   B: _____ they had one set for weekdays and another for Sundays and holidays.

    a. After   b. Before   c. Because

Indefinite Pronouns

Indefinite pronouns do not refer to any specific person or thing. Indefinite pronouns include *anybody, anyone, anything, each, everybody, nobody, nothing, no one, somebody,* and *someone*. These indefinite pronouns are singular and go with verbs in the singular form. Indefinite pronouns like *some* and *few* go with verbs in the plural form.

Pronoun	Explanation
Someone took my history book.	I don't know who took it.
I didn't like **anything** at that restaurant.	Use *anything* in a negative sentence: I tried different things at the restaurant and didn't like them.
We all had a piece of cake, and then there was **nothing** left.	We ate all the cake. No piece was left.
We loved the concert. **No one** left early.	Not one person left early.

For grammar reference, go to the Grammar Appendix.

D. Complete the conversation with words from the box.

someone	nothing	ago
anything	no one	

ALISON: Dad! I can't find my blue earrings. I took them from their box an hour ago. Are they on the table?

FATHER: No, there's (1) _____ here.

ALISON: Maybe (2) _____ took them.

FATHER: I don't think so. Didn't you leave them in your room?

ALISON: I can't remember (3) _____!

FATHER: Sweetie? (4) _____ took them. You're wearing them!

ALISON: You're right. I put them in an hour (5) _____ . I can't believe it!

Pair and Share

With a partner, ask and answer questions using indefinite pronouns.

Is anybody absent today?

No, . . .

Before Listening

A. Look at the pictures. What do you think the conversations will be about?

B. Listen to the first conversation. Then number the events in the correct order.

2 She washes clothes.

1 She works at the hospital.

3 She takes the bus home.

C. Listen to the second conversation. Then number the events in the correct order.

3 Aunt Nannan and Uncle Ju-Long moved into their own apartment.

1 Aunt Nannan lived at home with her parents.

2 Aunt Nannan married Uncle Ju-Long.

After Listening

D. Think about an interesting event that took place recently in your school. Share with a partner.

5 | Pronunciation

Informal speaking: Final *t* in *wasn't* and *weren't*

Sometimes when you speak, you say the words quickly and the sounds blend together. This is a form of informal speaking. When you say the words *wasn't*, *weren't*, *isn't* and *aren't*, you often blend the final *-t* sound with the sound at the beginning of the next word.

A. Listen to these sentences. Draw lines where the end of words with a final *-t* blend into the beginning of the next word.

1. There aren't many little children in my family.

2. There weren't a lot of people at the party.

3. Bill and Luke weren't tired after the game.

4. They aren't English; they're Scottish.

B. Listen to the audio and repeat.

 A. Listen to the conversation and complete the sentences. Then listen again and check your answers.

Dave: How has London changed since you were young, Grandpa?

Grandpa: Oh, it's much better now.

Dave: Better? (1) _____?

Grandpa: (2) _____ there is more work now, and less pollution. The economy was very bad when I was young. (3) _____ a lot of workers lost their jobs.

Dave: (4) _____ didn't you lose your job?

Grandpa: (5) _____ I worked with computer technology. It was a new field then. But they weren't like the ones we have today.

Dave: (6) _____ not? (7) _____ they were slow?

Grandpa: Yes, and they were a lot bigger, too. Computers today are small and light. (8) _____ they are so easy to carry.

B. Your Turn

Roleplay the conversation with a partner. How would Dave respond? Write your answer in the blank space.

Your idea: _____

_____

 C. Listen to the audio and take notes. Prepare to ask and answer questions about important events in your life.

Pair and Share

With a partner, ask and answer questions about important events in your life.

Where did you go to elementary school?

I went to New World Elementary School in Taipei.

Reading

Before Reading

A. Look at the pictures. Ask questions about the pictures starting with *where*, *when*, *what*, and *why*.

- Before reading a text, look at the pictures.
- Ask yourself questions about the pictures such as *Where was it taken?*, *When was it taken?*, *What is happening?*, or *Why did it happen?* to understand events and details better.

B. Read the text and underline details that describe how cities in Southeast Asia have changed.

Changes in Southeast Asia

Life in Southeast Asia has **changed** a lot over the last 40 years.

1. Traffic is a big **problem** today. Cities are getting bigger, and there are more and more cars. Roads are crowded, and the cars and motorbikes create pollution. People need other ways to get around. In Manila, Philippines, there is a system of elevated trains that travel **quickly** in the city. It is **cheap**, so millions of people use it. In Bangkok, Thailand, the Skytrain is a popular means of transportation. These elevated trains didn't **exist** 40 years ago.

2. **Malls** are very popular in many Asian cities. People **meet** friends there, go shopping, eat at restaurants, watch movies, or go ice skating. Many malls were built after 1990, and new ones go up every year. Some malls have parking space for thousands of cars.

3. More people live in cities, so daily life has changed. In Ho Chi Minh City, Vietnam, for example, there were quiet vegetable **markets** and parks. Today, people move fast and are always busy. Markets and parks are crowded and noisy.

How will life be different 40 years from now? City planners all over Asia are already thinking about the future.

After Reading

C. Answer the questions.

1. How did Manila solve the traffic problem?
2. Why are malls a good use of space?
3. How has Ho Chi Minh changed?
4. What kinds of changes do you see in the future?

D. Match the paragraph numbers to the pictures. Complete the chart by writing questions about each picture starting with *where*, *when*, *what*, or *why*.

Picture	Paragraph	Question
A		
B		
C		
D		

8 | Writing

Writing Strategy: Write topic sentences

Writing topic sentences helps you introduce the main idea of a paragraph.

A. Read and underline the sentence in each paragraph that best summarizes the entire paragraph. Where in the paragraph is it located?

Changes in Chicago in the Last 20 Years

_____.

Chicago is a fun and exciting city. It has so many things to see and do! There are many parks, restaurants, museums, and shows. The Art Institute, for example, is one of the best museums in the country. If you're a sports fan, you can check out a baseball game at Wrigley Field. There's always something interesting to do.

_____.

Many tourists come to the beautiful new convention center, or to the Lollapalooza music festival in Grant Park. Modern buildings attract visitors, too. These and many other attractions make Chicago a popular place to visit.

_____.

The city used to be very polluted. There was trash in the river and lake. There were too many cars, trucks, and factories. Now, the city is becoming very "green." Thousands of people ride their bikes. It's easy to recycle, too. There are special baskets where you can put glass, plastic, and paper. Chicago is more eco-friendly than it used to be.

B. Read again and write the topic sentences on the lines provided.

C. Write a topic sentence about your city. Then write a paragraph with details to support the topic sentence.

UNIT 6 — Giving Advice

In this unit, I will learn to . . .
- give and get advice.
- use different expressions to give advice.
- see the connection between main ideas and good titles.

1 | Get Ready

 Who do you usually go to for advice? Why?

A. Look at the pictures and read the text. What kinds of advice do parents and friends give to teenagers? Do they always listen? Why or why not?

When I was 14, I always wanted to grow up fast. I wanted to go dancing, have a boyfriend, and things like that. My mom said to me, "Don't hurry so much. Enjoy middle school first." That was the best advice she gave me! I was much happier taking it easy.

I was a quiet boy, but I wanted to be popular and good at sports. My best friend said, "You're a **nice** guy; you don't have to be popular. Be yourself." But I didn't listen! A few years later I learned to **accept** myself, and I felt much better.

I was a happy kid in middle school, but I used to spend a lot of time with my tablet. My parents didn't like that. They told me to play more sports and to socialize. I followed their **advice**, and I became a good volleyball player.

B. Complete the sentences using words or phrases from the box.

accept	take it easy	advice
grow up	middle school	yourself

1. Where did you _____?

2. In the U.S., _____ is for Grades 6, 7, and 8.

3. I only give _____ when somebody asks for it.

4. Don't work too hard and _____ .

5. It's fun to be _____ and show your true feelings.

6. You won't be very happy if you don't _____ yourself.

Pair and Share

Talk to a partner about giving and asking for advice.

> Who do you ask for advice? Why?

> I ask my mom for advice. She always knows what to do.

Ask and answer questions about good advice.

> What's the best advice you ever got?

> My dad told me that saving money is important. I think it's true.

A. In pairs, listen to the audio and talk about the best way to make friends.

Word Box

accept
advice
behave
embarrassed
give up
hygiene
judge
nice
no big deal
shy
sociable
take a shower

B. Match the words to their meaning.

1. shy	•	• act the right way
2. give up	•	• think of someone as good or bad without really knowing the person
3. embarrassed	•	• cleanliness
4. behave	•	• not important
5. hygiene	•	• feeling that other people are laughing at you or thinking bad things about you
6. judge	•	• enjoying the company of other people
7. no big deal	•	• stop trying
8. sociable	•	• feeling nervous and uncomfortable about meeting other people

 C. Choose the correct word from the box to complete the sentences. Then listen and check your answers.

1. When you're _____, it can be difficult to talk to people you don't know.

2. Many teens are _____ and like doing things in large groups.

3. It's important to know how to _____ in different situations.

4. Personal _____ is important because cleanliness and good health go together.

5. When you are kind to people, you help others and are _____ to them.

6. Many people feel _____ when they make mistakes in public.

7. You should accept people as they are; don't _____ them.

Used to

The expression **used to** indicates an action in the past that a person doesn't do anymore in the present.

Subject	Used to	Verb	Complement
I	**used to**	**spend**	a lot of time on my laptop.
She	**didn't use to**	**play**	many sports.

For grammar reference, go to Grammar Appendix.

A. Look at the pictures and circle T for *True* or F for *False*. Correct the false statements.

1. Frank used to play soccer when he was young.   T   F

_____

2. Susan used to dance ballet when she was young.   T   F

_____

Should / Shouldn't

We use **should** or **shouldn't** to express recommendations or give advice.

Question Word	Should	Subject	Verb	Complement
What	**should**	I	do	about my bad grades?
	Should	we	take	extra classes?

Subject	Should	Verb	Complement
You	**should**	do	your homework.
You	**shouldn't**	forget	to review your lessons.

B. Read the text and underline the expressions to give advice.

Understanding others

Humans are social by nature. It is important for us to understand the feelings of others. That does not mean being friends with everybody. It simply means putting yourself in another person's shoes.

Why should we do that?

When you understand others, you can make them feel better. When others understand you, you can share your ideas and feelings. People should be understanding and shouldn't criticize others.

How can we become more understanding?

Here are two tips:

1. *Really listen when someone talks to you*. You shouldn't interrupt, and don't judge the person or his or her opinion. Just listen first. How is the person feeling? What does he or she need or want?

2. *Talk to a person you don't know well*. You don't need to make a new friend, but you should try to understand him or her. You should be open to meet new people.

C. Choose the correct answers.

1. What is the main idea of the article?

   a. You should listen to others.
   b. You can learn to be understanding.
   c. You should talk more to your friends.

2. What idea is NOT in the article?

   a. You should look into a person's eyes.
   b. You shouldn't interrupt a person.
   c. You don't need to make new friends to be understanding.

3. What is NOT an example of being understanding?

   a. Listening carefully.
   b. Judging people.
   c. Talking to a person you don't know well.

4. What do you need to listen for?

   a. If the person likes you.
   b. If you understand the person's vocabulary.
   c. What the person feels and needs.

D. Complete the sentences with *should, shouldn't, used to,* or *didn't use to.*

a. When I was in primary school, I (1) _____ spend a lot of time on the computer.

b. My classmates (2) _____ play with the ball inside the classroom. They (3) _____ pay attention to the teacher.

c. Teenagers (4) _____ learn how to understand their emotions.

d. I (5) _____ take the bus to school but now I cycle.

Pair and Share

Work with a partner. Ask and answer questions with *used to*.

> What did you use to do a long time ago?

> I used to play with dolls. I don't do that so much anymore.

Ask for and give advice.

> I get tired a lot in the afternoon. What do you think I should do?

> Drink some water. That always wakes me up.

Listening Strategy:
Connect main ideas and good titles

Good titles always connect to the main idea of a story or article. Before reading or listening, look at the title. Guess what the story is about. After reading or listening, look at the title again. See if your guess about the main idea was correct.

Before Listening

A. Look at the pictures. They show two friends, Ben and Amber. What do you think the story will be about? Then choose the best title for the group of pictures.

A. Changing Habits   **B. Fitness is Fun**   **C. Good Advice**

B. Listen to the conversation and circle T for *True* or F for *False*.

1. Ben used to be late.	T	F
2. Ben didn't like to play sports.	T	F
3. Amber always exercised but never arrived on time.	T	F
4. Amber used to tell stories whenever she was angry.	T	F
5. They stopped running together.	T	F

After Listening

C. Write about an important lesson that you learned. Give your article a title.

5 | Pronunciation

The voiced and unvoiced *th-* sound

The *th-* sound can be pronounced in two ways: voiced (as in *the* and *that*) and unvoiced (as in *think* and *Thursday*).

A. Listen. Underline the words with voiced *th-* and circle the words with unvoiced *th-*.

1. Are these your things?
2. This morning the weather is nice.
3. There are thirty socks on the floor.

4. Do you think I should call them?
5. Don't throw that away.
6. You should thank your brother.

B. Listen to the audio and repeat.

 A. Listen to the conversation and complete the sentences. Then listen again and check your answers.

Mia: Natalie, I need your advice.

Natalie: OK. What's up?

Mia: I get seven dollars allowance a week, and I don't think it's enough.

Natalie: Seven dollars? I don't get any allowance.

Mia: Really? How do you buy your snacks then?

Natalie: I work. I do chores at home. Cleaning the refrigerator: one dollar. Washing the dishes: 50 cents. My parents won't just give me money. I have to do something. (1) _____ try doing some chores for money?

Mia: But . . . Don't you think I could ask my parents for a higher allowance?

Natalie: Well, you can try. But maybe (2) _____ do chores, too.

Mia: That's not the advice I expected.

Natalie: I know. But (3) _____ expect your parents will give you money without a reason. (4) _____ to talk to them. Tell them why you want more money.

Mia: That might help.

B. Your Turn

Roleplay the conversation with a partner. How would Natalie respond? Write your answer in the blank space.

Your idea: _____

_____

 C. Listen to the audio and take notes. Prepare to give some advice.

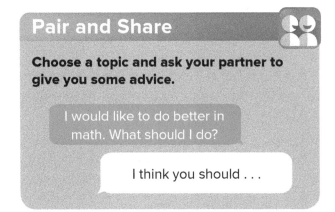

Pair and Share

Choose a topic and ask your partner to give you some advice.

I would like to do better in math. What should I do?

I think you should . . .

Reading

Reading Strategy:
Write titles and headings

Titles and headings tell readers about the main idea of a text.

• To write a good title, first find the main idea.
• Then, state the main idea in a few words to write a title.

Before Reading

A. In pairs, discuss these questions. Do you think people you don't know can give you good advice? Why or why not?

B. Read the text and underline key details in each letter to Dr. Lee.

 Dr. Lee's Advice Column

Teens often don't know *whom* to ask for **advice**. Here are three examples.

Dear Dr. Lee,
I'm in high school in Japan and I sleep all the time! I sleep in class and during self-study at night. The teachers are angry with me. I go to bed at 11 and wake up at 6:30. My friends say I should sleep more at night, but I have many activities. What do you recommend? —Brenda (17)

Dr. Lee: Brenda, you should see a doctor. Sleepiness can have a physical or emotional cause. You may be sick or stressed. You should make sure to sleep eight or nine hours every night.

Dear Dr. Lee,
I am Chinese, but I live in the U.S. Every summer, I go back to China to see my family. Last year, I met a Chinese-American girl, "Jane," in China. When I got back to the U.S., I couldn't contact her because I only knew her Chinese name. Later, a classmate (Jane's friend) told me Jane's English name. Now I want to add Jane to a social network. Will she **accept** my request? —Tommy (14)

Dr. Lee: Tommy, you should ask Jane's friend for advice. She knows Jane best. If she agrees, ask her to get in touch with Jane and see what happens.

Dear Dr. Lee,
My friends have helped their parents cook and clean since they were 12, but I don't do anything in the house. My parents always do everything for me. I'm so **embarrassed**! I want to go to college and live independently, but I don't know how to do anything! Help me! —Cora (17)

Dr. Lee: Cora, I think your friends and your parents can help you. Ask them to teach you, and ask them for advice. Don't **give up**! They will be happy to help you.

After Reading

C. Complete the chart. What advice does Dr. Lee give?

Name	Problem	Advice
Brenda	Sleeping during school	
Tommy	Adding someone to his social media network	
Cora	Not knowing how to do housework	

D. Work with a partner to write a title for each letter to Dr. Lee.

8 | Writing

Writing Strategy:
Write an email to give advice to a friend

- Write down your ideas in any order.
- Write a first draft of your email.
- Check logic, grammar, and spelling.
- Write a final draft.

A. In pairs, discuss these questions. What is bullying? Can you give some examples of bullying?

B. Read the paragraph and underline details about the problem.

Can you help me? I have a problem at school with a boy who doesn't like me. He makes fun of me and calls me names. I try to ignore him, but it's difficult. My classmates like me, but they are afraid of the boy. It started in private, but now he says these things in public, too. I feel terrible! What should I do? —Taylor

C. Write a letter giving advice.

Dear Taylor,

_____

_____

_____

_____

Use What You Know

ABC Vocabulary

A. Choose the correct word from the box to complete the sentences.

daughters	**impossible**	**sneakers**
happy	**middle**	**problem**

1. Lu is going running. She's putting on her _____ .

2. We are students in _____ school.

3. If you have a _____ , you can ask for advice.

4. Tess is a kind person; she's always making someone _____ .

5. It can be difficult to change your routines, but it's not _____ .

6. Our neighbors have a son and two _____ .

B. Circle the correct words.

1. I used to live in a house with my parents but now that I have my own job, I live in a small (market / apartment / restaurant).

2. I'm moving house next month and am packing up all my things. I didn't realize I had so much (advice / job / stuff)—I need more than ten boxes!

3. Bob and Cherie decided to go to the mall (yesterday / morning / meet) to shop and watch a movie.

4. Don't worry, it's (impossible / embarrassing / no big deal). You can always try again!

5. It's important to have good (shower / judge / hygiene) so that you won't get sick so often.

C. Find words that go together to form expressions. Then write three sentences.

be	**give**	**take**
best	**happy**	**up**
do	**it**	**your**
easy	**make**	**yourself**

_____

1. _____

2. _____

3. _____

Grammar

A. Complete the sentences with the correct past form of the verb in parentheses.

Tom: Hi, Carl. Guess what? My parents (1) _____ (buy) a new apartment!

Carl: Really? Do you like it?

Tom: Yes, it's nice. The old apartment (2) _____ (be) small, and this one is bigger. I (3) _____ (not / have) my own room, but now I do.

Carl: Cool! When (4) _____ you (5) _____ (move)?

Tom: I (6) _____ (paint) my room last Friday, and we (7) _____ (move) in on Saturday. I'm organizing a get-together at our new home next month. You're invited!

B. Complete the letter using words from the box.

someone	nothing	someone
no one	something	anything

Dear Marjorie,

You asked me, "What was life like before the Internet existed?" Well, here's my answer!

No online TV: You could only choose between the programs that were on at that moment. If you weren't home, (1) _____ had to record your program on a VCR (Video Cassette Recorder).

No quick information: You had to go to the library and look in books. (2) _____ could get information fast at home.

No online magazines: If (3) _____ liked an article, they made a photocopy of it.

No online banking: You couldn't buy (4) _____ from home instantly. You had to send a check by mail.

No online shopping: There was (5) _____ to buy instantly. You chose (6) _____ from a catalog, made a telephone call, and they brought you the item a week later.

I think life is better with the Internet!

Love,

Granny

a library

a clay tablet

Johannes Gutenberg

 ## Reading: History

 ### The History of Libraries

a papyrus scroll

When you think about a library, you probably imagine a place with books in bookcases. But libraries weren't always like that.

Before books **existed**, there were clay tablets. Five thousand years ago in Mesopotamia (now Iraq), there was a "library" of clay tablets.

The Ancient Egyptians used papyrus scrolls. They made their "paper" from a local plant. The Library of Alexandria was famous because there were scrolls about mathematics, astronomy, and many other sciences.

The Ancient Greeks copied their paper scrolls by hand—letter by letter, word by word. Because of this, scrolls were not **cheap** at all. Only very special people used libraries.

In the 14th century, some rich families had their own library of hand-written books. There were many libraries in Europe and the Middle East, and people took books from libraries to copy them. It was **impossible** for just any person to read in a library. Guests needed special permission.

Gutenberg made the first printing press around 1450, and the first printed books changed the world. It was possible to print large numbers of books **quickly**, and to distribute books to different cities and countries. There was just one **problem**: not many people could read at that time.

The first public library opened in the U.S. in 1833. After that, many people spent time doing **research** in libraries.

Now, what will the future bring?

A. Read and circle T for *True* or F for *False*. Correct each false statement.

1. Books always existed in the same form.   T   F

   _____

2. The Ancient Egyptians made scrolls from a plant.   T   F

   _____

3. All the Ancient Greeks took scrolls home to read.   T   F

   _____

4. For a long time, people copied scrolls by hand.   T   F

   _____

5. The first printing press was made in 1833.   T   F

   _____

B. Complete the sentences based on the reading.

1. _____ in Mesopotamia, there was a "library" of clay tablets.

2. The Library of Alexandria was famous for its scrolls about mathematics, _____.

3. In 14th-century Europe, to go to libraries, guests needed _____.

4. Gutenberg made the first printing press around _____.

C. Ask your partner these questions.

1. When was the last time you went to a library?

2. How is a library better than using the Internet to find information?

3. What did you learn from this text?

D. Investigate a library in your city and visit your school library. Write the differences in the chart. Then, answer the questions.

Local Library	School Library

1. How are the libraries different?

2. Which library do you prefer? Why?

3. Do you think libraries will disappear because of the Internet? Why or why not?

 **Project**

In this project, you will plan a roleplay of an important event in your life and record it. Use what you know from Units 4 to 6 to complete the project.

How does the past shape us?

Step 1 Plan

Think of an event in the past that has changed you.

Write what happened.	How did it change your life?

Step 2 Create

Create three to four drawings to show what happened.

Step 3 Rehearse

Work in groups of three to five and choose one of your stories.

Make a roleplay of the event.

Write the script. Look up unknown words in the dictionary.

Rehearse it.

Step 4 Record

Use your phone or tablet to record your roleplay.

Share with the class.

Creative Zone

1. List some common problems that teens may have.

_____

_____

_____

2. Roleplay

With a partner, choose a problem and prepare a roleplay. One student explains the problem and the other gives advice. Choose roles (friends, mother-daughter, doctor-patient, etc).

Script

A: _____   B: _____

A: _____   B: _____

A: _____   B: _____

3. Perform your roleplay for the class.

7 | Travel

8 | Collections

9 | Transportation

What can we learn through traveling?

 Look at the picture. Read the unit topics and answer the questions.

- **Where are they?**

- **Why are they happy?**

- **What do you think they are learning?**

CAN DO statements

After the next three units, you will be able to . . .

- talk about traveling.
- talk about collecting.
- talk about transportation.

In this unit, I will learn to . . .
- talk about traveling.
- give recommendations with a variety of structures.
- read and listen for causes.

1 | Get Ready

 Why do people travel?

A. Look at the pictures and read the passage below.

Ada is from Hong Kong. She always wanted to study business. But during a vacation to the Three Gorges Dam in Yichang, she changed her mind. Now she is studying engineering, and she's happy. She wants to work in a **foreign** country, maybe Thailand.

José is from Guatemala City. One year, he **explored** the Mayan Ruins in the rainforest with his family. Now he loves to see the interesting people, the old towns, and the mountains. He takes **trips** on the weekends with his family. There's so much to see at just a short **distance** from the city!

Mark is a businessman from Brussels, Belgium, who wanted to work in another country. He traveled to Ecuador because he was interested in the country. In the **capital** Quito, he met Paola, a young businesswoman. Mark and Paola are starting a bakery next year, and they are going to get married.

B. Read and circle T for *True* or F for *False*. Correct the false statements.

1. Ada changed her study plans while on vacation.   T   F

   _____

2. José learned to love his country by traveling.   T   F

   _____

3. José normally visits the capital, Guatemala City.   T   F

   _____

4. Mark and Paola live in Belgium.   T   F

   _____

5. Mark and Paola are going to get married.   T   F

   _____

Pair and Share

Ask and answer about traveling.

What places do tourists like to visit in our country?

They visit . . .

Ask and answer the question about yourself.

Do you like to travel?

Yes, I like to visit . . .

A. Listen to the audio and read along. Guess the meaning of the words in bold.

Many people like to travel. Some travelers take walks and travel **slowly**. They take their time to **explore** nature.

Other people like to travel **fast**. They go **abroad** and visit many countries in a short time. They cover long **distances** when they travel.

Whether you travel slowly or fast, you need to be **safe**. Keep to the main tourist areas and don't be outside late at night. Keep your credit cards, **passport**, and **visa** in the hotel if you don't need them.

Also, travelers should travel light and not have too many bags and **suitcases**.

Word Box

abroad	passport
capital	safe
distance	slowly
explore	suitcase
fast	trip
foreign	visa

B. Complete the sentences using the words from the box.

Before you travel (1) _____, you need to plan your (2) _____ carefully. Firstly, you need to have a (3) _____, and in some countries, you may need to have a (4) _____. Secondly, you need to plan your transportation and find a place to stay. When you visit a (5) _____ country, you have the opportunity to meet new people, taste new foods, and (6) _____ new places. You can travel (7) _____ and take your time; or you can travel (8) _____ and see many places in a short time.

C. Match the words to their definitions.

1. foreign	•	•	not quickly
2. trip	•	•	from another country
3. safe	•	•	a document that allows you to travel to other countries
4. capital	•	•	outside your country
5. slowly	•	•	without danger or risk
6. fast	•	•	the city where the government of a country is
7. visa	•	•	quickly
8. passport	•	•	a journey to a place
9. abroad	•	•	a special permit to travel into a country

Should / Why don't you . . . ?

Should + verb expresses a recommendation. **Shouldn't** is used to express a negative recommendation.

Example: *When the weather is bad, you **shouldn't swim** in the ocean; you **should stay** in the hotel.*

Why don't you + verb . . . ? or **Why doesn't he / she** + verb . . . ? is also used to express a recommendation.

Example: **Why don't you** *play ping-pong at the hotel?*

You can use different structures to give recommendations:

Structure	Example
should	You **should eat** healthy food on vacation, too.
shouldn't	You **shouldn't eat** junk food every day.
Why don't you	**Why don't you order** a salad?
You can	**You can have** some pasta, too.

*For grammar reference, go to Grammar Appendix.

A. Look at the pictures and complete the sentences.

French fries

sushi

milk

1. You _____ eat fast food. 2. You _____ eat fish. 3. _____ have some milk?

B. Complete the sentences using *should, shouldn't, why don't you,* and *you can.*

1. You _____ run near the pool. You might slip and fall down.

2. _____ come to my house tomorrow. We can watch a movie.

3. _____ go there? It's a great place for a vacation.

4. You _____ always look before you cross the road.

5. He _____ eat so much. It isn't good for his health.

6. We _____ be late. We might miss our flight.

Let's

Let's + verb is used at the beginning of a sentence to make an invitation.

Example: **Let's go** to the movies.

C. Write invitations for the actions below.

1. take a vacation _____

2. go to the mountains _____

3. stay in a hotel _____

4. order vegetarian food _____

Have to / Had to

Have to or **had to** + verb is used to express an obligation in the present or past tense.

Example: *You **have to plan** your trip carefully.*

Example: *She **had to renew** her passport.*

An obligation is stronger than a recommendation.

D. Rewrite these sentences using *have to* or *had to*.

1. It's necessary to take your passport.

   _____

2. It was necessary for me to get a visa.

   _____

3. It was necessary for him to go to the capital.

   _____

4. It's necessary for us to study a foreign language.

   _____

Go + verb + ing

The structure **go + verb + ing** is used to talk about physical leisure activities.

Example: *go camping, go swimming*

E. Underline the expressions that use *go* + verb + *ing*.

1. Let's go surfing this summer.

2. Why don't you go running on the beach?

3. We wanted to go swimming, but the water was too cold.

4. Many tourists go dancing at night in one of the big hotels.

5. You can go cycling in the forest.

Pair and Share

Invite a classmate to do something with you.

Let's go cycling in the park later!

Sure, that sounds like fun!

Ask and answer about obligations.

What do you have to do every day?

I have to . . .

Before Listening

A. Look at the picture. Where are these people? What are they doing?

To understand *why* something happens, listen for the words *why* and *because*.

• *Why* often comes in questions.
• *Because* often comes in sentences describing a reason.

B. Listen and put the events in order. Listen again and check your answers.

_____ The flights were delayed because of the snow.

_____ Sonia and her family went on vacation in Los Angeles.

_____ John called his boss.

_____ They had to change planes in New York.

_____ Their plane took off.

_____ They went to a hotel.

After Listening

C. What do you like and dislike about traveling by plane? Share with a partner.

 5 | **Pronunciation** 🎤

Word Stress

Important words in a sentence can be stressed or emphasized. Because of this, the word stress may change the meaning of a sentence.

A. Listen and underline the words and phrases that are stressed.

1. Let's explore the city tomorrow morning.

2. You have to get a new passport.

3. The red suitcase is mine.

4. I don't like to travel long distances.

5. Do you think it's safe to walk here at night?

B. Listen to the audio and repeat.

Speaking Strategy:
Ask people to repeat slowly

Examples:

- *I'm sorry. I'm just learning English. Could you repeat that?*
- *Could you repeat that slowly, please?*
- *Could you speak more slowly, please?*

 A. Listen to the conversation and complete the sentences. Listen again and check your answers.

Ms. Lozano: Hello. My flight is Air New Zealand 006. Where do I (1) _____ to go?

Agent: Oh, the flight to San Francisco is boarding already. It's at Gate 17. You'd better hurry, ma'am.

Ms. Lozano: I'm sorry, could you repeat that (2) _____, please?

Agent: Sure. Your airplane is at gate number 17. I'll take you there. (3) _____ go!

Ms. Lozano: Do we have to walk (4) _____?

Agent: Yes, the passengers are getting on the plane (5) _____.

Ms. Lozano: Oh dear. (6) _____ you so much!

Agent: (7) _____ problem, ma'am. We've arrived!

Ms. Lozano: Is there time to (8) _____ something to eat?

B. Your Turn

Roleplay the conversation with a partner. How would the agent answer the last question?

Your idea: _____

_____

 C. Listen to the audio and take notes. Prepare to ask someone to speak slowly.

Pair and Share

Ask and answer a question for information. Then ask the person to repeat it slowly.

Excuse me . . . ?

It's . . .

Could you repeat that slowly, please?

Sure . . .

Before Reading

A. Look at the pictures and guess where they were taken.

Water is needed.

Building the pump.

Fresh water!

B. Read the article. Underline the causes and circle the effects.

🔊 **Building Pumps in Africa**

by Tyler Simmons (15)

1. On our last vacation, my parents and I traveled **abroad** to Tanzania in East Africa. We wanted to help the people there because many towns don't have **safe** water. They need water for drinking, cooking, farming, and for their animals.

2. First, we contacted an organization in Tanzania. A man from the organization informed us about a town that needed a water pump. He also sent a description of the land. With this information, my father started planning the work. Everybody in my family participated: my father, my mother, and me.

3. My father is an engineer; he knows about the technology. He took lessons to learn Swahili online because not all people in Tanzania speak English. Most of them speak Swahili, but there are many other languages in the country.

4. My mother and I raised money for the project because the equipment is expensive. I gave a presentation at school and collected money. My mom wrote an article and raised money online. We paid for our plane tickets, we got **passports** and **visas**, we packed our **suitcases** and left.

5. When we arrived in Tanzania, the work started. Our contact took us to the little town. The equipment was already there. My father taught the local people how to build the pump. When it was working, the townspeople were very happy because they had fresh water!

6. Now, I am in an organization for teens, and next year I am going to participate in another project in Tanzania. I am learning Swahili online because I want to communicate with the people there. It feels wonderful to help others!

After Reading

C. Choose the best title for each paragraph.

_____ In Tanzania	_____ My plans for future projects
_____ Planning and preparation	_____ My father's responsibilities
_____ Introduction	_____ My mother's and my participation

D. Answer the questions.

1. Why did Tyler go to Tanzania?

_____

2. Why did his father learn Swahili?

_____

3. Why did they need to get money for the project?

_____

4. Why did Tyler start learning Swahili too?

_____

8 | Writing

A. Work with a partner. Imagine where you would like to go on vacation and what kinds of activities you would do there.

B. Read the postcard. Take note of the kind of information you need to write a postcard. Note where all the parts are.

Writing Strategy:
Write a postcard

- Choose or make a picture for your postcard.
- Write the recipient's name and address on the right.
- Start with a salutation.
- Write about your experiences on the left.
- Finish with a closing and your name.

Hi Mike,

My family and I are in Rome, Italy. It's an incredible city. I learned a lot about the ancient Romans. They ate lying down! We also went swimming at a beach near Rome, but the water was cold. I prefer our own beaches!

See you soon,
Kayla

Mike Alberts

1288 Linden Ave.

Ourtown, FL

32826 USA

C. Write your own postcard using your information from Activity A.

In this unit, I will learn to . . .
- talk about collecting.
- use possessive pronouns.
- listen and read for specific details.

1 | Get Ready

 Why do people collect things?

 A. Look at the pictures and listen to the audio. What do these people collect?

B. Answer the following questions about the collectors.

1. Why does Lois feel that hot sauce bottles are easy to collect?

_____

2. What Pokémon stuff does Frank have only a few of?

_____

3. How many phones does Thomas have in his living room?

_____

C. Match the sentence parts.

1. Thomas collects	•	•	cheap.
2. He has	•	•	cell phones.
3. Lois kept	•	•	the hot sauce bottles she liked.
4. Hot sauce bottles are	•	•	too expensive for Frank.
5. Rare action figures are	•	•	a hundred of them in his living room.

Pair and Share

Ask and answer the question about the text.

How many phones does Thomas have?

He has a hundred phones.

Ask and answer the question about yourself.

What do you collect?

I collect cell phone cards.

A. Listen to the audio and read along. Guess the meaning of the words in bold.

Here are five tips for people who want to start collecting!

Tip 1: Select a specific theme.
If you want to **collect** shells, don't **add** other items to your collection. **Include** only shells.

Tip 2: Ask other collectors questions.
Many collectors will be happy to **show** you their collections.

Tip 3: Think about money.
If the **price** of every object in your theme is high, it's difficult to form a collection. **Rare** objects are probably **expensive**.

Tip 4: **Compare** prices.
Choose things that are **cheap**, or buy what you **prefer**.

Tip 5: **Keep** collecting fun!
Take your time. As you **grow up**, your collection can grow with you.

Word Box

add	include
cheap	keep
collect	prefer
compare	price
expensive	rare
grow up	show

B. Match the words to their definitions.

1. add	•	• get older, become an adult
2. price	•	• maintain something in the same way
3. rare	•	• put something with a group of things
4. expensive	•	• special, not common
5. keep	•	• the money you pay for something
6. grow up	•	• the opposite of cheap

C. Complete the sentences using words from the box.

To start a collection, you should think about the money you want to spend. You should (1) _____ objects to your collection regularly, but you should also (2) _____ prices when possible. You can (3) _____ both cheap and (4) _____ objects, but you shouldn't buy too many (5) _____ things because they cost too much. Most importantly, you should enjoy (6) _____!

Possessive Pronouns

Possessive pronouns show ownership and are usually found at the end of the sentence or clause. Possessive pronouns replace the possessive adjective and the noun.

Possessive adjective	Possessive pronoun
It's **my** dog.	It's **mine**.
It's **your** dog.	It's **yours**.
It's **his** dog.	It's **his**.
It's **her** dog.	It's **hers**.
It's **our** dog.	It's **ours**.
It's **your** dog.	It's **yours**.
It's **their** dog.	It's **theirs**.

For grammar reference, go to Grammar Appendix.

A. Look at the pictures. Write a sentence for each one using a possessive pronoun.

1. _____

2. _____

3. _____

B. Underline the possessive pronoun in each sentence.

1. My brother and I share a room. The bed on the left is his.

2. Their school is in the suburbs; ours is in the city.

3. This isn't mine. It's yours!

4. The roses in the neighbors' garden are red, and ours are white.

5. Olga has two cats, and this kitten is hers, too.

6. These are their books. They're theirs.

Pronouns: *One / Ones*

Use the pronouns *one* and *ones* to refer to objects that were mentioned before. *One* is used in singular and *ones* in plural.

Example: *I like blue and green sweaters. This green **one** is my favorite. These blue **ones** are new.*

C. Read the sentences and circle the correct pronoun.

1. Ceramics are fun to collect. These (one / ones) are from Egypt.

2. Do you like the red car or the green car? I like the red (one / ones).

3. I collect toy robots. This (one / ones) is my favorite.

4. These are some of my stamps. This (one / ones) from Australia is beautiful.

5. Many people collect baseball cards. Old (one / ones) can be very expensive!

D. Read and answer the questions about yourself. Use *one* or *ones*.

1. Do you write with blue or black pens?

_____

2. Do you have a new or an old cell phone?

_____

3. Do you have a small or a large family?

_____

Too + adjective

Use ***too* + adjective** to emphasize that something is excessive. *Too* is often used to express a negative idea.

E. Complete the sentences with words from the box.

boring	far
big	expensive
difficult	

1. Carla is a comic book collector. She trades comics with boys because it's too _____ to find girls who collect them.

2. Carla lives in a town. The comic stores are too _____ away, so she buys comics online.

3. She doesn't have a lot of money, and many comics are too _____.

4. She doesn't like black-and-white comics. She thinks they're too _____.

5. Carla has about 200 comic books. Her parents say her collection is getting too _____ for her room!

Pair and Share

Ask and answer questions about possessions.

Are these your pens?

Yes, they're mine.

Is this Tina's book?

No, it isn't hers.

- Listen for a general understanding.
- Read the questions that ask for specific information.
- Listen again and pay attention to the details.

Before Listening

A. Look at the picture. What is the girl doing? What objects can you see?

B. Listen to the text and answer the questions. Listen again and check your answers.

1. What is Jenna's problem?

_____

2. Who can she give things away to?

_____

3. What is the second tip?

_____

4. What is the third tip?

_____

5. What things should she throw in the trash?

_____

After Listening

C. How can you be better organized? Share with a partner.

---

5 | Pronunciation

Short *a*, long *a*, -*r* controlled *a*, -*l* controlled *a*

The letter *a* can have different sounds. You need to recognize and practice the sound for each word.

A. Listen. Check (✓) the words with the correct sound.

1. **Short *a*, as in *hat*:** [ ] cap, [ ] make, [ ] Pat, [ ] map

2. **Long *a*, as in *cane*:** [ ] same, [ ] plane, [ ] late, [ ] apple

3. ***-ar* as in *car*:** [ ] tar, [ ] par, [ ] care, [ ] far

4. ***-al* as in *ball*:** [ ] tall, [ ] whale, [ ] already, [ ] call

5. **Short *a*, as in *hat*:** [ ] that, [ ] cat, [ ] sat, [ ] ate

6. **Long *a*, as in *cane*:** [ ] face, [ ] state, [ ] game, [ ] ant

B. Listen to the audio and repeat.

Speaking Strategy:
Describe objects and ownership

You can describe an object's: color (red, yellow); size (big, small); shape (round, triangular); age (new, old); and material (plastic, metal).

You can describe ownership with possessive adjectives and pronouns (my, mine).

 A. Listen to the conversation and complete the sentences. Listen again and check your answers.

Ms. Lewis: Do your children collect things?

Mrs. Tann: Yes, Simon and Gwen both have a coin collection. (1) _____ contains only British coins, and (2) _____ are from all over the world.

Ms. Lewis: Do they have favorite pieces?

Mrs. Tann: Yes, they do. Gwen's favorites are (3) _____, (4) _____ Chinese coins. Simon's favorite coin isn't exactly (5) _____; it's a 12-sided three-penny coin.

Ms. Lewis: How interesting; I thought all coins were the same!

B. Your Turn

Roleplay the conversation with a partner. How would Mrs. Tann respond?

Your idea: _____

_____

 C. Listen to the audio. Take notes to prepare to ask about what is in your partner's room.

Pair and Share

Ask and answer about what you have in your room.

What do you have in your room?

I have . . .

What's your favorite . . .?

It's . . .

Reading Strategy:
Read for specific ideas: Nouns

When you look for specific ideas in a text, read the nouns carefully.

• Nouns can be subjects (the doer of the action).
• Nouns can also be objects (receiving the action).

Before Reading

A. Look at the picture and describe the woman. Is she more like an adult or a child?

B. Read the text and underline the nouns.

 Meet a Kidult

Kidults are adults who **prefer** to live like young people. Kidults aren't ready to be responsible adults. They generally live with their parents, participate in activities for teens, and dress like teens.

May Zhang loves being a girl. She is 22 years old, but she feels 14. May thinks adults are serious and boring. She says, "If you **compare** adults and children, children are always happier." She **keeps** teddy bears and toys, and she works in a little store in Jalan Besar in Singapore. She **adds** toys from the store to her own collection. May lives at home with her parents and does not want to marry and have children.

May told us, "My favorite area in the city is Little India. It's a magical place, full of color. And I love the "supertrees" in one of the gardens at night. When you see them, you feel like Alice in Wonderland. Everything is possible." May's mother told us what she thinks of May's lifestyle. "At first, my husband and I wanted May to **grow up** and be responsible. But now I accept and like her as she is. May will become an adult when she's ready."

C. Read the text again and complete the sentences.

1. Kidults are adults that behave like _____.

2. May thinks _____ are happier than adults.

3. May collects _____.

4. She works in a _____.

5. May likes to visit the _____.

6. May's _____ accepts May's lifestyle.

After Reading

D. Read the sentences and circle T for *True* or F for *False*. Correct the false statements.

1. According to the text, kidults are children who behave like adults.　　　T　　F

_____

2. According to the text, kidults don't want to grow up.　　　T　　F

_____

3. According to the text, kidults are unhappy.　　　T　　F

_____

8 | Writing

A. Think of a topic or a collection that you can describe. Draw a few items below.

**Writing Strategy:
Write descriptions**

Using descriptions makes your writing more interesting and helps to form a picture in the reader's mind. Look out for the color, size, shape, and material of the object and describe it.

B. Read the text and underline the description words.

I have a collection of jeans in my room. Some are mine, but most were from family or friends. Jeans can be blue, black, or even interesting colors like yellow or green! They are all made of "denim," a kind of cotton. Some are small and short and others are big and long. Some have zippers, but I like the ones with buttons. My favorite pair is one that my grandpa gave me. They are blue, big, and ugly. I like them because my grandpa wore them when my mother was just a little girl!

C. Write a description in your notebook using your ideas from Activity A.

In this unit, I will learn to . . .
- talk about transportation.
- use comparatives and superlatives.
- listen and read for the author's purpose.

1 |　Get Ready

 What kind of transportation do you use most often?

A. Look at the pictures. How are these people traveling?

People prefer to travel in different ways. Let's look at three options.

Linda Yi is from China. She likes to travel by train. She loves meeting new people on the train and talking to them. Linda also likes to take photos of the countryside as she travels by train. She can sleep and travel at the same time. Linda thinks it's exciting to wake up in a new place in the morning!

Mr. and Mrs. Weber from Germany love traveling by **cruise** ship. They like the food, the activities, and the trips on land. It's so **easy** to travel by cruise ship: you don't have to plan anything. A cruise ship is more **comfortable** than a hotel! The Webers think it's the **best** option.

Australian Tom Gould doesn't like to be a **passenger**; he prefers to drive. When he travels around Australia by car, he can choose where to go and when to stop. Tom can sleep in his car. He says it's the cheapest and most comfortable option.

**B. Read and circle T for _True_ or F for _False_.
Correct the false statements.**

1. Linda likes to travel by plane.　　T　　F
_____

2. Linda enjoys sleeping on a train.　　T　　F
_____

3. The Webers love to go on a cruise.　　T　　F
_____

4. Traveling on a cruise takes a lot　　T　　F
of planning.
_____

5. Tom Gould thinks it's cheap to travel　　T　　F
by car.
_____

Pair and Share

Ask and answer questions about the text.

Why does Linda Yi like to travel by train?

She likes to meet new people.

Ask and answer questions about transportation.

What means of transportation do you like? Why?

I like . . . because . . .

A. Listen to the audio and read along. Guess the meaning of the words in bold.

Bicycles and cars are **common** means of transportation. Bikes are cheap and **easy** to ride. Cars **cost** a lot of money. You need to be 18 to drive a car, and bikes are **suitable** for all ages. Cars may be more **comfortable**, but bikes provide a good form of exercise.

You can also be a **passenger** on a train, a **cruise** ship, or an airplane. You can often enjoy **incredible views** when you look out the window. An **airline** can offer you a window seat if you ask for it. It is the **best** form of travel, especially to other countries. But the cheapest form of travel is **backpacking**.

Word Box

airline	cruise
backpack	easy
best	incredible
comfortable	passenger
common	suitable
cost	view

B. Match the words to their definitions.

1. cost	•	• usual, typical
2. view	•	• have an amount of money to pay
3. suitable	•	• better than all the other options
4. common	•	• the landscape you see
5. incredible	•	• really beautiful or good
6. easy	•	• right for you
7. best	•	• simple

C. Complete the sentences using words from the box.

1. Jim takes his books to school in his _____.

2. Lee loves traveling on a _____. She likes ships and the sea.

3. Cars are more _____ than bikes.

4. Delta Airlines was the biggest _____ in the world in 2014. They had 129 million _____!

5. A cruise _____ a lot of money, but the cabins (rooms) are really comfortable, and the
   food is _____—it's so delicious!

Comparatives

Use descriptive adjectives to make comparisons. When the word *than* is used, the form of the adjective changes.

One-syllable adjectives usually use *-er*. *Trains are **faster than** buses*.

Two- or more syllable adjectives usually use *more* before the adjective. *Plane tickets are **more expensive than** bus tickets*.

A. Complete the sentences using the correct form of the adjective.

Adjective	Comparative sentences
old	1. The buses are _____ the trains in my town.
cheap	2. These sneakers are _____ those.
tall	3. Duane is _____ Mike.
comfortable	4. I think a train is _____ a car.
suitable	5. A backpack is _____ for school than a handbag.
expensive	6. Flying is _____ traveling by car.

Spelling Changes

Double the consonant for short adjectives ending in consonant + vowel + consonant:

*bi**g** > bi**gg**er*; *ho**t** > ho**tt**er*

Adjectives ending in *y* change to *-ier* in the comparative form:

*happ**y** > happ**ier***; *eas**y** > eas**ier***

B. Look at the picture. What is she thinking about?

Pair and Share

Ask and answer questions about school subjects.

What's the most interesting school subject for you?

It's . . . because . . .

Ask and answer questions about singers.

Who's the best singer in our country?

I think it's . . . because . . .

C. Look at the pictures and make comparisons.

Amber

Destiny

1. Amber is _____ (young) than Destiny.

2. Destiny is _____ (tall) than Amber.

3. Destiny has _____ (strong) muscles than Amber.

4. Amber looks _____ (relaxed) than Destiny.

5. Destiny is _____ (focused) than Amber.

D. Complete the sentences using the comparative form of the word in parentheses.

1. Luke thinks American football is _____ (exciting) than soccer.

2. Harry looks _____ (happy) than his sister.

3. Do you really think math is _____ (interesting) than English?

4. *The Little Prince* is _____ (short) than *The Secret Garden*.

5. Gillian thinks ping-pong is a _____ (fast) sport than tennis.

Superlatives

The superlative is used to talk about one thing only, unlike comparatives which take two things and compare them against each other. Superlatives express the idea that someone or something has the most of a particular quality within a group. The word *the* is always added before the superlative in a sentence.

*bi**g** > the bi**gg**est*; *ho**t** > the ho**ttest***
*happ**y** > the happ**iest***; *eas**y** > the eas**iest***

E. Complete the sentences so they are true for you.

1. I think _____ is the most exciting sport to play, and _____ is the most interesting sport to watch.

2. _____ is the best means of transportation for me.

3. _____ is the happiest person I know.

4 | Listening

Before Listening

A. Look at the pictures. How safe or dangerous are these alternative forms of transportation? Why do you think so?

The speaker's purpose can be:

- to persuade: convince the listener of the speaker's opinion.
- to inform: give the listener new information.
- to entertain the listener.

 B. Listen to the audio. What is the speaker's purpose? Listen again and check your answer.

The woman on the radio wants to: _____

1. **persuade** the listener that these different forms of transportation are fun but possibly dangerous.

2. **inform** the listener about the three most common means of alternative transportation.

3. **entertain** the listener with some fun information, but she doesn't give her opinion.

After Listening

C. What's your favorite form of transportation? Share with a small group.

5 | Pronunciation

Final *-th*

When the letters *th* appear at the end of a word, the sound is unvoiced, just like the words *math* and *bath*.

 A. Listen. Circle the sound you hear.

1. boss / both
2. toes / tooth
3. five / fifth

4. rude / Ruth
5. eight / eighth
6. math / mat

 B. Listen to the audio and repeat.

A. Listen to the conversation and complete the sentences. Listen again and check your answers.

Akira: Dad, can I go to school by myself? I'm old enough now.

Father: (1) _____. I think you're too young. I prefer to take you.

Akira: I (2) _____, (3) _____ I can take the sky train. It's faster than going by car.

Father: (4) _____, (5) _____ driving is safer.

Akira: OK. (6) _____, Dad.

B. Your Turn

Roleplay the conversation with a partner. How would the father respond?

Your idea: _____

_____

 C. Listen to the audio and take notes. Prepare to agree or disagree respectfully.

Pair and Share

Roleplay a conversation between a parent and a teen. Agree or disagree respectfully.

Mom / Dad, can I . . . ?

I think . . .

Reading Strategy:
Read for main ideas: Author's purpose

The author's purpose can be:

• to persuade: convince the reader of the author's opinion.
• to inform: give the reader new information.
• to entertain the reader.

Before Reading

A. In pairs, look at the picture and discuss these questions. Where is this airport? Is it large? Is it expensive? Is it in a famous city?

B. Read and underline the benefits of low-cost airlines.

 Low-Cost Airlines

by Frank Lewis

Low-cost **airlines** are companies that offer **cheap** flights to certain places. For example, in the 1990s, it **cost** about $200 to travel from Bangkok to Singapore by plane. Nowadays, you can find a cheap flight for less than $50! These prices make air travel a **suitable** means of transportation for many people. It can also bring more tourists.

Because the cost is lower, many more people fly now compared to 20 years ago. Low-cost airlines are making air travel **easier** for more travelers. Today, it is possible for almost anyone to fly to another country; in the past that wasn't possible.

The first low-cost airline was Southwest Airlines in the U.S. It offered flights between the cities of Houston, Dallas, and San Antonio in the state of Texas. Then, more low-cost airlines appeared in the U.S. and the rest of the world, especially in Europe and Asia. Today, they are **common** everywhere and they compete with regular airlines.

Why are low-cost airlines cheaper? Regular airlines offer many services that make traveling **comfortable**, but expensive. With low-cost airlines, extra services are not included in the price. On many low-cost flights, **passengers** pay for food and drinks, or they pay extra for every suitcase. Low-cost airlines usually go to the most important cities, so they may not fly to all the places that regular airlines do.

After Reading

C. Check (✓) the correct information in the chart.

Features	Regular airline	Low-cost airline
1. Tickets can be expensive.	✓	
2. Passengers may pay more to bring a suitcase.		
3. They serve food for free.		
4. They normally fly to the largest cities.		
5. They make it possible for more people to travel.		

D. Answer the questions.

1. What is the author's purpose? _____

2. How do you know? _____

8 | Writing

**Writing Strategy:
Write concluding sentences**

A concluding sentence comes at the end of the paragraph. It restates and reinforces the main idea of the paragraph, so it is often similar to the first sentence of the paragraph.

A. Read and choose the correct picture.

The train is a very common means of transport in Japan, but tourists often get confused. There are so many rules! Commuter trains are the most complicated. Tickets are sold at ticket machines, so you need to know exactly where you are going. There's usually a map above the machines. Travelers can also buy a train pass. Local trains stop at every station, rapid trains stop at some stations, and then there are express and limited express trains. When you are at a platform, check that your train is going in the right direction.

B. Choose the correct concluding sentence.

1. Japan Rail Pass is a great option for travelers.

2. Taking a commuter train isn't easy for tourists in Japan.

3. Japan is a great country for fast train travel.

C. Read and write a concluding sentence.

The Orient Express is a legendary train that runs from Bangkok to Singapore. It is famous for its great luxury. Chefs prepare excellent food on the train. Passengers can sleep in a comfortable bed in their private cabin. The views are incredible and the service is excellent.

The Orient Express is _____

ABC Vocabulary

A. Complete the sentences with words from the box.

expensive	safer	easier
includes	suitable	price

Climbing walls are artificial walls that you can climb. A climbing wall is (1) _____ to climb than a mountain, and it is (2) _____ because there are "grips" for your hands and feet. The tallest climbing walls are only (3) _____ for experienced climbers. The (4) _____ to climb a wall normally (5) _____ your safety gear: a harness and a helmet. Climbing a big wall can be (6) _____, but many climbers say climbing a wall is an incredible experience.

B. Answer the questions using the words in parentheses.

1. Do you like hamburgers? (*prefer*)

   _____

2. What sports do teens play in your city? (*common*)

   _____

3. Where can you eat good food? (*best*)

   _____

4. What is an important city in your country? (*capital*)

   _____

5. What would you like to do when you're older? (*grow up*)

   _____

C. Write sentences using these words.

1. grow up _____.
2. collect _____.
3. easy _____.
4. incredible _____.
5. abroad _____.
6. explore _____.

Grammar

A. Circle the correct word in each sentence.

1. If you are not sure about something, you (should / suggest) ask your teacher to explain it again.

2. Mike's sister is still too young to travel on her own. He (has / have) to take her to school.

3. We went (dance / dancing) on Saturday evening.

4. Let's (play / playing) another game tomorrow.

5. Is this (your / yours) pencil box? No, it's not (my / mine).

6. Do you like those dogs? I think they're OK, but I prefer this brown (one /ones).

7. This soup tastes bad! It has (too / many) much salt!

B. Complete the sentences using the correct possessive adjective or pronoun.

1. My bedroom is blue; what color is _____?

2. Naoko has her tablet, and Harry has _____ book.

3. **Eileen:** Do you have any dogs?

   Sandy: Yes, we have two. _____ dogs are Bobby and Blacky.

4. We live on a nice street, but _____ house doesn't have a large garden.

5. Our teacher is Ms. Willis, but there's another English class next door. _____ teacher is Mr. Tumaru.

6. Your new shoes are so nice! I should get a new pair soon. _____ are getting old.

C. Complete the questions using the correct form of the adjective. Then answer the questions.

1. Which is _____ (good) for you: studying at home or studying at school? Why?

   _____

2. What is _____ (comfortable) for you: sleeping on a bed or on a sofa? Why?

   _____

3. What is _____ (easy) for you: playing a team sport or playing video games? Why?

   _____

4. Which classroom has the _____ (good) view in your school? Why do you think so?

   _____

Reading: Literature

Robinson Crusoe

Robinson Crusoe is the title of a famous book from the 18th century. A young Englishman named Robinson Crusoe goes **abroad** without telling his parents. Some years later, he is on a ship in the Atlantic Ocean, and the ship sinks. Robinson reaches an island, but all the other people on the ship die. Robinson does not find other people on the island, so he has to build a house and find food. He lives alone, but he is quite **comfortable** and has an **easy** life. It takes him many years to organize his house and his lifestyle.

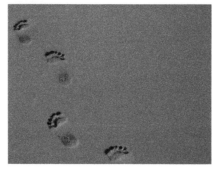

One day, Robinson finds footsteps on the beach. There is another person on the island! Robinson is happy and afraid at the same time. Later, he finds a group of cannibals. They have a prisoner, and Robinson helps the man escape. He calls the man Friday. After 28 years on the island, a ship takes Robinson back to England.

The story continues with more adventures, but the most popular part of the book is where it describes how Robinson finds ways to survive on the island. He learns to be independent and **safe**.

The book starts with, "I was born in the year 1632, in the city of York." This makes the reader think Robinson wrote the story about his life. In reality, the character Robinson was an invention. The author of the book was Daniel Defoe.

There are many books, movies, and TV shows about Robinson Crusoe's **incredible** story because people like to imagine what it is like to survive on an island.

A. Read the sentences and circle T for *True* or F for *False*. Correct the false statements.

1. *Robinson Crusoe* is the name of a book.   T   F

   _____

2. Robinson's parents sent him abroad.   T   F

   _____

3. He helped Friday escape from the cannibals.   T   F

   _____

4. Robinson stayed on the island for more than 25 years.   T   F

   _____

5. Robinson wrote the book.   T   F

   _____

B. Write three more questions about the text. Then ask and answer the questions with your partner.

1. _____

2. _____

3. _____

C. Write a short conversation between Robinson Crusoe and Friday.

RC: _____

F: _____

RC: _____

F: _____

RC: _____

D. Write the names of some old stories or books that are still popular now.

E. With a partner, choose one book or story. Then complete the chart.

Question	Robinson Crusoe	Our story: _____
1. Did the story really happen?	no	
2. Can you learn a lesson from the story?	yes	
3. Is the story told from parent to child?	no	
4. Can a similar story take place in modern times?	yes	
5. Are there modern movies and TV shows about the story?	yes	

Project

In this project, you will interview people to find out what we learn through traveling. Use what you know from Units 7 to 9 to complete the project.

What can we learn through traveling?

Step 1 Plan

Complete the chart about your travels. If you haven't traveled much, you can answer about a person you know.

Places you visited	Activities you did	Food you ate	Things you saw

---

Step 2 Interview

Interview an adult who has traveled abroad recently. Ask these questions:

- Where did you go?
- What did you do?
- What did you learn about the place?
- What did you learn about the people?
- What did you learn about yourself?

Step 3 Create

Get into groups of three.

Make a poster showing what people learn when they travel.

Use images and words.

Creative Zone

Poas Volcano, Costa Rica

Cappadocia, Turkey

Brainstorm

A. Work in groups. Choose a country or city for a vacation.

Write notes about the place.

The volcano is white , It's amazing. It's a very good spot
for look that. She is in a cave with an amazing vue, all is
green and you cee a little village on the top of the
moutain.

_____

_____

_____

Planning

B. With your classmates, write down what you can see and do in the place you choose.

_____

_____

_____

_____

_____

_____

Presentation

C. Prepare an advertisement for the place. This can be a TV commercial or an Internet promotion. Present it to your classmates.

How can we help each other?

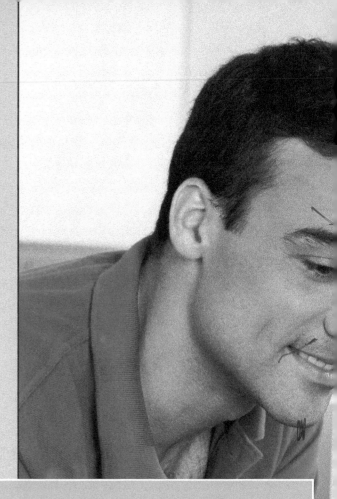

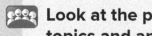 Look at the picture. Read the unit topics and answer the questions.

- Why is this young man helping this woman?

- When did you last help someone?

- How should we help each other?

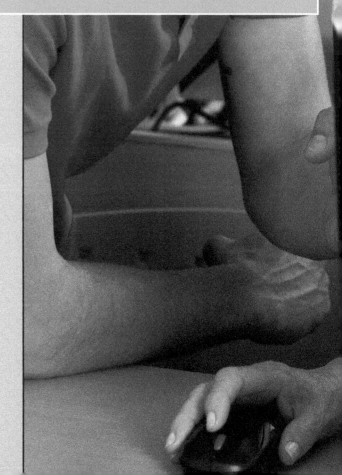

CAN DO statements

After the next three units, you will be able to . . .

- talk about helping others and working as a volunteer.

- talk about requests.

- describe people's lives.

In this unit, I will learn to . . .
- talk about helping others and working as a volunteer.
- use *will* and *going to*.
- listen and read for the main idea.

1 | Get Ready

Why is helping others important?

 A. Look at the picture and read the text. What do volunteers help out with? What is a community center? Listen to the audio.

Min and Gun were born in the United States, but their parents came from Korea. Min and Gun are volunteers at a **community** service center in Los Angeles. The center is an **organization** that helps Korean immigrants in the United States. This is **necessary** work, but the volunteers are not paid a salary.

Min speaks and reads English and Korean and helps Korean immigrants. Min is 14 years old, and she likes to work with kids. Some immigrants have young children that don't speak English. Min works at the center every Wednesday afternoon.

Min's brother Gun is studying accounting at California State University, Los Angeles. Gun helps Koreans with paperwork, for example, with their yearly tax returns. His "clients" are happy with Gun's work. Paperwork helps Korean immigrants **improve** their situation.

Gun believes that the new immigrants **need** a lot of help, but there are not enough volunteers to help them.

B. Read and circle T for *True* or F for *False*. Correct the false statements.

1. Min and Gun's parents arrived in the U.S. from Korea.   T   F

   _____

2. Min likes children.   T   F

   _____

3. Gun is 14 years old.   T   F

   _____

4. Gun works as an accountant at the university.   T   F

   _____

5. There are enough volunteers to help the new immigrants.   T   F

   _____

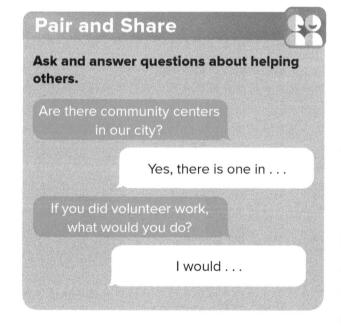

Pair and Share

Ask and answer questions about helping others.

Are there community centers in our city?

Yes, there is one in . . .

If you did volunteer work, what would you do?

I would . . .

A. Listen to the audio and read along. Guess the meaning of the words in bold.

Tom: Hi, everybody! Today, Gwen and I will be talking about being **kind**.

Gwen: For example, helping your parents is a way to show them **respect**. You can also be **generous** to your brothers and sisters by sharing your things with them.

Tom: Older and sick people often have a need for help. For example, it's **useful** if you go shopping for a sick person.

Gwen: Exactly. Many people **believe** that you should do a good deed every day. You can improve a person's life and be a source of **happiness** just by doing something small. Have you helped others **recently**?

Tom: Let's listen to some music, and we'll be back.

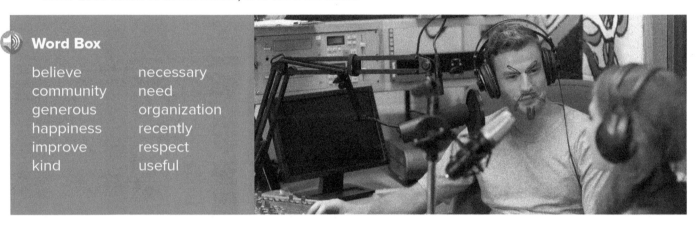

Word Box

believe	necessary
community	need
generous	organization
happiness	recently
improve	respect
kind	useful

B. Complete the sentences using words from the word box.

Tom: Hi, everybody! Today we're talking about being (1) _____.

Gwen: Right, Tom. For example, you can do (2) _____ things for your family: clean the floors, wash the dishes, or prepare breakfast on a Saturday. These are all (3) _____ chores.

Tom: Very true, Gwen! When you help people in your family, you make them happy. This (4) _____ then comes back to you.

Gwen: Yes! Or maybe you can do some volunteer work in your (5) _____, or you can be (6) _____ with a donation to an (7) _____ that needs money.

Tom: Helping others is easy! Let's listen to some music, and we'll be back. This is the latest song . . .

C. Match the words from the box with the correct definitions.

1. respect	•	• think something is true or correct
2. need	•	• make better
3. recently	•	• something necessary for a person to have
4. improve	•	• not long ago
5. believe	•	• a feeling for someone who you think highly of as a result of their abilities or qualities

Will for future

Use **will** + verb to express the future tense. For a negative idea, use **will not** or **won't**.

The auxiliary *will* is the same for all persons: *I will play, she will listen, they will learn*. The negative form is *won't*.

	Examples with time expressions
affirmative	He *will cook* dinner **on Saturday**.
negative	They *won't sing* songs in Spanish class **tomorrow**.
Yes / No questions	*Will* you *study* grammar **tonight**?
Wh- questions	Where *will* they *go* to high school **next year**?

For grammar reference, go to Grammar Appendix.

She *will teach* her cousins to make pizza.

She *will help* her brother with his homework.

She *will learn* how to change a tire.

A. Complete the sentences with a logical time expression for the future.

1. Will you do your homework this afternoon or _____?

2. Janine won't go to the movies with us _____.

3. I'll go to high school _____!

4. I'd like to be an astronaut _____.

5. We'll go to the market _____ because we don't have any tomatoes.

B. Complete the sentences using *will / won't* and the verbs from the box.

buy	do	eat	help
harvest	plant	prepare	pull

Gerald's family has a community garden: a vegetable garden that isn't close to their house. A community garden is a lot of work, and everybody needs to help. The family divided up the tasks for next month:

Mr. Brown will clean the land. His wife and Gerald (1) _____ him. Mr. Brown (2) _____ (not) it alone.

Mrs. Brown (3) _____ some tomato seeds at the store with Jim, Gerald's little brother.

But Mrs. Brown (4) _____ (not) the seeds in the garden; Jim will do it.

The family has carrots in their garden that are ready to harvest. Gerald (5) _____ the carrots.

Jim (6) _____ some lettuces out of the ground. Mrs. Brown (7) _____ salads with the vegetables for many days.

And who (8) _____ the salads? They all will!

Be going to to express future

Be + going to + verb can also be used to express that something will happen in the future:

Are you **going to donate** money to the Red Crescent?
Yes, but I'**m not going to give** a lot this time. I'**m going to donate** five dollars.

Will and **going to** can express different intentions. *Will* is often used to make an offer or a decision in the moment, and to make a prediction:

I'**ll help** you with that task (right now).
It **will rain** today!

Going to is used to express a planned decision:

I'**m going to help** my grandmother after school tomorrow.

C. Complete the sentences using *going to* and the verb indicated.

Arav: Hey, Vivan, (1) _____ you
(2) _____ (go) on vacation?

Vivan: No, I'm not. I (3) _____ (work) as a volunteer in an animal shelter.

Arav: Really? Where (4) _____ you
(5) _____ (do) that?

Vivan: Here, in Jaipur! There are many abandoned animals that live on the streets—mostly dogs, but also monkeys and birds.
I (6) _____ (help) feed the animals and find them a new home.

Arav: Is there a hospital, too?

Vivan: Yes, but I (7) _____ (not/work) there. If I see blood, I faint! Actually, my sister (8) _____ (help) at the hospital. She wants to be a vet.

Pair and Share

Ask and answer questions about helping others.

How do you normally help in your family?

I normally help . . .

Who are you going to help later?

I'm going to help . . .

Listening Strategy:
Listen for the main ideas

• Listen to the complete audio once. Don't worry about understanding all the details.
• Listen for the most important idea.
• The main idea is normally repeated.

Before Listening

A. Look at the pictures. How are the people in the pictures feeling?

 B. Listen to the audio. Then choose the correct main idea.

Helping and giving to others _____

1. makes you feel good too.

2. doesn't cost any money.

3. is something you can do at school.

 C. Listen again and number the pictures in the order you hear them.

After Listening

D. When did you last help somebody? How did you feel afterwards? Share with a partner.

5 | **Pronunciation** 🎤

Silent -t

Some words have a "silent *t*" where the *t* sound is not pronounced.

Example: *Did you **lis[t]en** carefully?*

 A. Listen to the audio and circle the word that has a silent -*t*.

1. Many Americans celebrate Christmas; but there are other winter festivals too.

2. You need to fasten your seat belt when you're sitting in the car.

3. There's a beautiful bird outside, and it's singing. Listen!

4. Do you often watch scary movies?

B. Listen to the audio and repeat.

Speaking Strategy:
Show support and offer help

• Offer help: *What's the matter? Do you want to talk about it? Can I help?*
• Show you are listening by nodding and saying: *Yes. Right. I'm so sorry. That's terrible. How awful.*
• Rephrase what the other person said to show that you understood.

 A. Listen to the conversation and complete the sentences. Listen again and check your answers.

Trish: Kayla, you look upset. (1) _____?

Kayla: I feel terrible. I lost my new jacket.

Trish: (2) _____?

Kayla: My mom gave me a new jacket for my birthday last month, and I lost it. When she finds out, she'll be so angry with me! Trish, I don't know what to do.

Trish: (3) _____. (4) _____?

Kayla: Well, maybe we can look for the jacket together.

Trish: Yes, let's do that. But right now we need to get to class. Come on, Kayla!

Kayla: You're right, let's go.

B. Your Turn

Roleplay the conversation with a partner. How would Trish respond?

Your idea: _____

_____

 C. Listen to the audio and take notes. Prepare to talk about an imaginary problem.

Pair and Share

Ask and answer questions about an imaginary problem.

. . . , you look upset. What's the matter?

I have a problem . . .

That's awful. Can I help?

Maybe you can . . .

Reading 📖

Reading Strategy:
Read for the main idea

• Read the text quickly.
• Don't worry about understanding all the details.
• Find the most important idea.
• The main idea is normally in the title and the first and last paragraphs.

Before Reading

A. Look at the picture and discuss the questions. Is everybody generous? Why or why not?

B. Read the text. Underline the title and the main idea in the first and last paragraphs.

 ### A Culture of Giving

Every year, the Charities Aid Foundation finds out which countries are the most **generous**. Southeast Asian countries usually rank pretty high. In fact, Myanmar came in first place.

What Is Generosity?

Generosity is the act of being **kind** to others and giving more than is needed. Simple acts of generosity include giving your seat to an older person on a bus, helping others, or donating time or money to a good cause. Charities Aid Foundation asks people from around the world three questions to determine how generous a country is.

1. Have you given money to charity in the last month?

2. Have you volunteered in the last month?

3. Have you helped a stranger in the last month?

Ninety-two percent of the people in Myanmar responded that they have **recently** donated money. Many people are quite surprised because they **believe** that only people in wealthy countries normally donate money. Myanmar is one of the poorest countries in the world, but its people more frequently donate money than people from the wealthiest countries. Thailand came in second place in this category, scoring 87 percent.

Cultural Belief

Why is helping others an important part of Myanmar's culture? Actually, this cultural belief is important in many countries in Southeast Asia. In some countries, people believe that what you do in this life will affect your next life. But in Myanmar, Thailand, Cambodia, and Laos, there is a strong culture of giving. People don't give because they have to, but because they want to help those in **need**. They believe giving will bring you **happiness**.

After Reading

C. Complete the sentences.

1. The Charities Aid Foundation found that Myanmar is _____

2. An example of an act of generosity is _____

3. Myanmar is a poor country, but 92 percent _____

4. People in Myanmar donate money _____

5. People in Southeast Asia believe that _____

D. Write the main idea of the text in your own words.

_____

_____

8 | Writing

A. Work with a partner. Choose a value that is important in your society. Describe it in one sentence.

Writing Strategy:
Plan a paragraph

- Decide on the main idea of your paragraph.
- Write a summary sentence.
- Then add details.

B. Read the text below. Look at the main idea and the supporting details. Discuss how they fit into the paragraph.

Equality is an important American value.

- People of different ethnic backgrounds are equal.
- Everybody's participation is valued in meetings and discussions.
- The boss listens to everybody.

Equality is an important American value. Equality means that people are equal, regardless of their ethnic backgrounds. Everybody's participation is valued in meetings and discussions. The boss listens to everybody. It's not the boss who tells the workers what to do; the boss is a participant, too.

C. Write a paragraph using the information you discussed in Activity A.

_____

_____

_____

_____

_____

_____

In this unit, I will learn to . . .
• talk about requests.
• use *want, tell, ask* and other structures for requests.
• read and listen for inferenced requests.

1 | **Get Ready**

 What do people often wish for?

A. Look at the pictures and answer the questions. Then listen to the audio.

1. Are these events happy or sad?

2. What do you think they are celebrating?

Dying Wishes

Some people make a special **request** when they are going to die. Here are three cases.

Brett Marie Christian was 15 and dying of leukemia. She lived in a hospice, a hospital for dying people. Before her **death**, she had one request: to have a formal dance party at the hospital. Brett Marie wore a pink dress and danced with her friend, Treyton. She died three days later.

Pete Hodge loved to fish in a river. One year he got very **sick**. Before he **died** at 61, he told his family about his dying **wish**. He said, "Make my ashes into bait to catch fish, and throw the bait into the river." A friend made 15 kilos of bait with corn and Pete's ashes. Pete's family then threw the bait in the river.

Wing-Yu from Hong Kong had a special wish when she was ill: she wanted to have a birthday celebration in a theme park. But she was so sick that she couldn't go. Fortunately, later she got better. She celebrated her 17th birthday in Disneyland.

B. Read and circle T for *True* or F for *False*. Correct the false statements.

1. Brett Marie had the party she wished for.   T   F

_____

2. Pete's hobby was fishing.   T   F

_____

3. Pete's friends and family didn't want to follow Pete's request.   T   F

_____

4. Wing-Yu died before her wish came true.   T   F

_____

Pair and Share

Ask and answer questions about requests.

What was the most unusual request on this page?

I think . . . because . . .

Ask and answer questions with your personal ideas.

Do you have a special wish?

Yes, I would like to . . .

2 | Vocabulary ABC

 A. Listen to the audio and read along. Guess the meaning of the words in bold.

Do you want to make the world a better place? You may think it's difficult to do because you cannot change important things, like **crime**, **violence**, or **poverty** in your city. But you can live in **peace** and be nice to a **sick** person, for example. You can do **favors** for people when you see they need help, not only when they have an **illness**. You can also do things to help the natural **ecology** of the Earth. Small actions make a difference, and you may leave the world a nicer place for the people around you.

Word Box

crime	peace
death	poverty
die	request
ecology	sick
favor	violence
illness	wish

B. Complete the sentences using words from the box. Then listen and check your answers.

When you ask people what they (1) _____ for, they often ask for (2) _____. People want the (3) _____ and (4) _____ in their cities and neighborhoods to end. Also the end of (5) _____ is a frequent (6) _____: people need some money for food, housing, clothes, education, and so on. People also wish for health because when you are (7) _____, you're less happy. People also don't want their relatives to (8) _____ when they are sick. Finally, people wish for a healthy relationship between nature and humans: the natural (9) _____ of Earth.

C. Match the words to the correct definitions.

1. favor	•	• a kind act that you do for someone
2. illness	•	• behavior that hurts someone or damages things
3. peace	•	• a disease that makes a person sick
4. poverty	•	• the state of being poor
5. violence	•	• a desire for something to happen even though it may not be possible
6. wish	•	• the opposite of violence; no war or fighting

Can / Could to express possibility

Can and **could** is used to express possibility in the present and past.

Examples:

*On some TV shows, contestants **can win** big prizes.*

*My dad **couldn't go** to the supermarket after work; he didn't have time.*

A. Complete the sentences using *can, can't,* **or** *could.*

In the past, you (1) _____ buy CDs of all your favorite bands. You (2) _____ do that anymore. Many CDs came with a booklet where you (3) _____ read the lyrics of the songs. You (4) _____ only buy complete albums. Nowadays, you (5) _____ buy individual songs on the Internet, which is cheaper, and you (6) _____ listen to them immediately.

So what do you prefer? CDs or downloading songs?

Will / Would to express possibility

Use **will** when you think something will happen.

Example: *I think it **will rain** this afternoon, so let's take our umbrellas.*

Use **would** in the past to say what you thought would happen.

Example: *I thought it **would rain**, so I took my umbrella.*

B. Read the sentences and circle the correct words.

1. I brought more money. I thought the restaurant (will / would) be more expensive.

2. It's 7:30. Do you think there (will / would) still be tickets for the 8 o'clock show?

3. There are many journalists at the hotel. They are hoping that the president (will / would) give a press conference.

4. It's late; we need to go. We (won't / wouldn't) have time to shower before going to school.

5. The organizers told me that there (will / would) be a break for lunch.

Want / Tell / Ask **for requests**

When you want to report a request, a verb like ***want / tell / ask*** is used with a *to* clause. The pattern is *want / tell / ask*, the object (receiver of the action), and an infinitive form of the verb.

Subject	Want / tell / ask	Object	Infinitive	Complement
I	**asked**	my mom	to give	me permission to go to the movies with my friend Li.
My mom	**wanted**	me	to send	her a message when we arrived at the mall.
She	**told**	me	to return	with Li's parents.

For grammar reference, go to Grammar Appendix.

C. Put the words in the correct order.

1. My father / the dishes. / me / wanted / to wash

   _____

2. my sister / to lend me / I / her cell phone. / asked

   _____

3. told / for Tuesday. / The teacher / to do the homework / us

   _____

4. to come / Leo / his friends / asked / to his birthday party.

   _____

5. Jasmin / with her. / wanted / me / to have lunch

   _____

Let / Will **to show intentions**

Use ***Let me*** and ***I'll*** to show your intention to do something immediately.
Example: ***Let me help*** you! ***I'll take*** that heavy bag!

D. Write sentences using *Let me* or *I'll*.

1. You see a boy who is carrying a lot of books and papers. He wants to open a door, but he doesn't have any free hands. What do you say?

   _____

2. An old woman has difficulty walking. She wants to cross the street, but she is afraid of the traffic. What do you say?

   _____

Pair and Share

Ask for and show your intention to help.

Can you help me carry this?

Sure. Let me help you.

Ask and answer about possibilities.

Do you think it will rain tomorrow?

No. I think the weather will be sunny.

Listening Strategy:
Make an indirect request
or suggestion

Before Listening

A. Look at the pictures. What do you think the people are asking?

There are many ways to make requests and suggestions in conversation. Sometimes you make a request indirectly:

- *Perhaps you should* do it again. (Direct = Could you do it again?)
- *You might consider* doing it tomorrow. (Direct = Would you do it tomorrow?)
- *It might be a good idea to* go to the store and buy some apples. (Direct = Please go to the store and buy some apples.)

B. Listen to the audio. Then answer the questions. Listen again to check your answers.

1. What subject does Dayna have a problem with?

   _____

2. What is Elsa's recommendation?

   _____

3. What is Miguel's problem?

   _____

4. What is the solution that Miguel likes?

   _____

After Listening

C. A friend of yours has lost a lot of money. Make four indirect suggestions about what he / she can do. Share them with a partner.

1. Maybe you should _____

2. You might consider _____

3. It might be a good idea to _____

4. Perhaps you should _____

5 | **Pronunciation**

Short *o* vs long *o*

The letter *o* has two main sounds: long as in *boat*, and short as in *pop*. Also some letters like *l* and *r* can influence the sound, for example, *l* in *old* and *r* in *or*.

A. Listen to the audio. Check (✓) the word you hear.

1. [ ] got   [ ] goat
2. [ ] off   [ ] oaf
3. [ ] slop   [ ] slope
4. [ ] not   [ ] note
5. [ ] rot   [ ] wrote
6. [ ] bought   [ ] boat

B. Listen to the audio and repeat.

 A. Listen to the conversation and complete the sentences. Listen again and check your answers.

Kylie: Cooking is fun! Cooking is so fun!

Brooke: Listen, great cook. (1) _____ me, please?

Kylie: I *am* helping! I went to the market with you.

Brooke: Yes, but now we need to cook. We promised Mom and Dad! (2) _____ those zucchini? And (3) _____ the oven to 150 degrees.

Kylie: Alright. What's next?

Brooke: I don't understand these instructions. (4) _____ them?

Kylie: OK, (5) _____ the cookbook. This is going to be a long evening . . . What if we ordered pizza?

B. Your Turn

Roleplay the conversation with a partner. How would Brooke answer the last question?

Your idea: _____

_____

Pair and Share

Make a direct request for something from your parents.

Can I stay out late on Friday night?

Well, let me think about it . . .

Make requests to work together with a partner at school.

Could you . . . ?

Sure, no problem.

C. Listen to the audio. Take notes and prepare to make requests.

Reading Strategy:
Make a request through inference

Making indirect requests requires the reader to infer what you want him / her to do. This is usually a polite way of asking someone to do something. For example:

- A man might email a friend: *Do you think you could help me paint these walls?*
- What he really means is: *I need you to help me paint these walls.*

Before Reading

A. Look at the pictures. Match the names with the countries.

Fernanda Jimenez, Colima	• •	Italy 
George Batenga, Dar es Salaam	• •	Mexico 
Giancarlo Rossi, Rome	• •	Tanzania 

🔊 **B. Read the emails. Underline the key sentences that use inference to make a request.**

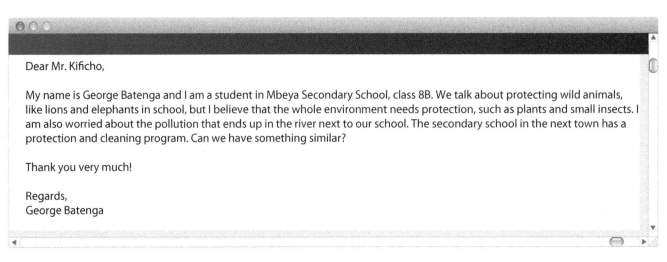

Dear Mr. Kificho,

My name is George Batenga and I am a student in Mbeya Secondary School, class 8B. We talk about protecting wild animals, like lions and elephants in school, but I believe that the whole environment needs protection, such as plants and small insects. I am also worried about the pollution that ends up in the river next to our school. The secondary school in the next town has a protection and cleaning program. Can we have something similar?

Thank you very much!

Regards,
George Batenga

Hi Aunt Lina,

How are you? When we watch the news about what's happening in the city, we worry about you and your cousin Pablo. It looks like there is a lot of crime, poverty, and violence in the capital. Here in our town, life is peaceful and quiet. My parents and I live here in peace and without worries. We have space in our house and two empty bedrooms. Why don't you come and stay for the weekend? Maybe you will like it here.

Please think about it!

Fernanda

After Reading

C. Answer the questions.

1. Does your school have programs to protect the environment? Explain your answer.

2. Does your city have a problem with crime or poverty? Explain your answer.

8 | Writing ✏

Writing Strategy:
Make a formal request

- Remember to keep the language formal and polite by making indirect requests.
- Give reasons for your request.

A. Work with a partner. Circle the reasons for the request in the email.

○○○

Giancarlo Rossi
Via San Martino 75, 00015
Rome, Italy

Dear Sir or Madam,

Last month, my friend Andrea Marino and I both bought a XOC soccer ball in Monterotondo. Three days later, both Andrea's soccer ball and my own were broken. There were too many leaks and we couldn't repair them. We went back to the store, but the employee told us there was nothing he could do.

I would like to ask you for a new soccer ball to replace the one I bought.

I am looking forward to your answer.

Respectfully,
Giancarlo Rossi

B. Underline all the words which are too informal in the following email.

○○○

Hi Mister,

Last week, my mother bought two packs of CHICKEY Frozen Tandoori Chicken and she made them for dinner. We ate it, and we all got sick. Medicine was expensive. We want to know what you plan to do about this.
I am expecting your answer soon.

Bye,
Thomas

C. Rewrite the email and make it more formal. Use the email in Activity A as an example.

Stories

In this unit, I will learn to . . .
- describe people's lives.
- use the present perfect and simple past tenses.
- listen and read for people's intentions.

1 | Get Ready ◐

Why are stories important to us?

🔊 **A.** Look at the pictures and listen to the audio. Why are these people heroes?

Chuck Feeney is a successful businessman and a philanthropist. He lives simply with a motto "Giving while living."

Eight-year-old **Michael Bowron** is very **brave**. His father got into an accident and both of them were **hurt**. He followed his father's instructions and managed to get them **rescued**.

🔊 **B.** Listen again and answer the questions.

1. Why do you think Feeney was an example for Bill Gates?

   _____

2. What does "giving while living" mean?

   _____

3. Why is Michael a hero?

   _____

4. What might have happened if Michael hadn't been brave, but afraid?

   _____

Pair and Share

Ask and answer questions about the biographies.

> Who do you admire more: Mr. Feeney or Michael Bowron?

>> I admire . . . because . . .

Ask and answer questions about another selfless hero.

> Do you know about another hero?

>> Yes, . . .

🔊 **A. Listen to the audio and read along. Guess the meaning of the words in bold.**

Last week, a nurse named James Wilburn **rescued** three people in a car accident. He was standing in **line** at a cinema downtown when there was a car accident. He **realized** that he had to act quickly. **Together** with another man, he **tried** to get the people out of the car while someone else **contacted** an ambulance. They were very **brave**. James said he **decided** to become a nurse after reading the **biography** of American poet and nurse Walt Whitman. Now James is **planning** to become an emergency nurse. His city is **promoting** a program to find more nurses for the city hospital.

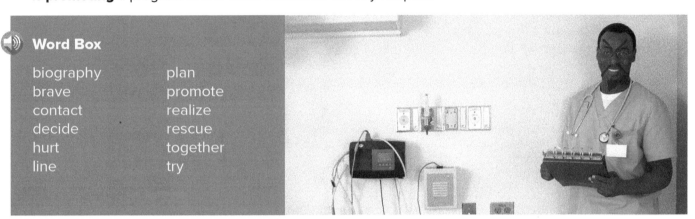

🔊 **Word Box**

biography	plan
brave	promote
contact	realize
decide	rescue
hurt	together
line	try

B. Complete the sentences using words from the box.

1. I don't like to stand in _____ to buy movie tickets; I prefer to buy tickets online.

2. Laura only had one pair of blue jeans. She _____ she wanted to get a new pair.

3. Did you read the _____ of Dr. Martin Luther King, Jr.?

4. Julian fell off his bike and got _____ badly.

5. When her little brother fell into the river, Hanna jumped in and saved him. She was very _____.

6. I went to school with one brown sock and one black one! I didn't _____ they were different.

7. We like to have large family dinners on Saturday; it brings the family _____.

C. Match the sentence halves.

1. Firefighters rescue	•	• her activities for the week.
2. We can try	•	• take care of sick people.
3. We are promoting	•	• the police when he got home.
4. Together they help us	•	• people from fires.
5. He contacted	•	• fire prevention.
6. On Sunday, Noemi planned	•	• to work on the project together.

Present Perfect

The **present perfect** is used to describe these two situations:

An action that started in the past and is still going on:
*Dillan **has lived** in Springville **all his life**.* (He *still* lives there today.)

An action that happened at an unknown time in the past:
*Dillan **has traveled** to New York **three times**.* (We don't know *when*.)

The present perfect is formed using *have* and the past participle of a verb. There are regular and irregular forms of past participles. Regular verbs use the same form for the simple past and past participle.

The charts below explains how to use the present perfect in the negative, and question forms.

Auxiliary *have*	Subject	Verb in past participle	Complement
Have	you	(ever) **watched**	that movie?
Has	Carla	(ever) **been**	to Hawaii?

Subject	Auxiliary *have*	Verb in past participle	Complement
Janine	**has (not)**	**gone**	to the gym every day this week.
Daniel and Bill	**have (not)**	**taken**	guitar lessons since first grade.

For grammar reference, go to Grammar Appendix.

A. Look at the picture and read the title. Guess what the text is about.

The Story of Martin Parsons

Firefighters are **brave** men and women who risk their lives to save others. Let's take Lieutenant Martin Parsons from Cape Town, South Africa, for example. He has worked as a firefighter for 20 years. He has been in numerous fires and has probably saved over 100 lives.

Martin believes that it's just as important to prevent fires. He has visited hundreds of classrooms to talk about the dangers of using fire. Martin likes to think he has prevented hundreds of fires, just by talking to kids.

B. Read the text again and underline examples of the present perfect.

Present Perfect vs Simple Past

The **present perfect** is used when you don't know when an action happened, or when an action started and is still going on. The **simple past** describes actions that started and finished in the past.

He **has donated** over 7 billion dollars so far.
(The action of donating money is still going on.)
He **made** his first million dollars as a co-inventor.
(We know the action finished in the past.)

C. Read and circle the correct form of the verbs.

Jennifer Clark is a jazz and pop singer from Chicago. She 1. (was / has been) a professional singer for 12 years. She 2. (started / has started) when she was 19 years old. She 3. (sang / has sung) jazz music since 2003. She 4. (won / has won) the Chicago Jazz Contest in 2008. Jennifer's greatest hit is "Summertime." This album 5. (sold / has sold) 200,000 copies in the last 10 years. Jennifer 6. (had / has had) some health problems last December, but now she is preparing a world tour, so you can listen to this great artist live!

D. Complete the conversation using the correct form of the verbs.

Min-soo: Have you ever (1) _____ (grow) your own vegetables?

Lisa: No, I haven't. My family has always (2) _____ (buy) our vegetables in the store. Plus, we don't (3) _____ (have) a garden.

Min-soo: Well, my family doesn't (4) _____ (have) a garden either. We have a small terrace where we grow tomatoes and herbs.
We've (5) _____ (have) tomatoes there since 2014. Remember when you (6) _____ (eat) spaghetti with tomato sauce with us last week? Those (7) _____ (be) our tomatoes.

Lisa: Really? That's interesting. Who (8) _____ (teach) you guys how to grow vegetables?

Min-soo: Nobody; you just have to buy the seeds. If you follow the instructions, you don't (9) _____ (need) a teacher. It's that easy!

Lisa: Cool! I'll (10) _____ (tell) my parents about it.

Pair and Share

Ask and answer questions about firefighters.

Why are firefighters heroic?

Because . . .

Ask and answer questions about your week so far.

Have you . . . this week?

Yes / No, I . . .

Listening Strategy:
Infer the reasons for situations or actions

Sometimes a speaker doesn't give a reason for situations or actions. Listen and make inferences about why things happened without the speaker's explanation. Ask: *"Why did he / she do this?"* Listen for clues.

Before Listening

A. Look at the pictures. When do people give baskets with food?

 B. Listen to the audio. Choose the correct answers. Listen again to check your answers.

1. Why was Tony's family poor?

   a. because his father didn't have a job

   b. because they spent all their money

   c. The article doesn't say.

2. What did the man at the door want to do?

   a. sell something

   b. give the family food

   c. stop the parents' fight

3. When did Tony start giving food to the poor?

   a. at age 11

   b. at age 17

   c. The article doesn't say.

4. Why are there tears in Tony's eyes when he tells this story?

   a. He remembers his parents' fight.

   b. He remembers not having food for Thanksgiving.

   c. He was changed by the man at the door.

After Listening

C. Infer the answers to these questions. Share your answers with a partner.

1. Why did Tony cry when he saw the food at the door?

2. Why did he cry when the man gave them the food?

5 | **Pronunciation** 🎤

Informal speaking: *was*

The past form *was* is often unstressed and the vowel sound is changed to a schwa sound /ə/.

 A. Listen to the audio. Write *a* when you hear *was* or ə for *wəs*.

1. Was it hot in Seoul yesterday? _____

2. Mrs. Lewis was early this morning. _____

3. I think it was last Tuesday. Yes, it was! I remember now. _____

 B. Listen to the audio and repeat.

 A. Listen to the conversation and complete the sentences. Listen again and check your answers.

Ali: HI, Ray. How was your weekend?

Ray: Not so good. Our dog was sick.

Ali: Oh no! (1) _____?

Ray: He wasn't eating. We had to take him to the vet on Saturday.

Ali: (2) _____?

Ray: Yes, it usually means he's sick. The vet gave us some medicine. We were planning to go to the movies, but that didn't happen.

Ali: I see. (3) _____.

Ray: But with the medicine, my dog seemed much better on Sunday.

Ali: Wow! (4) _____ worked fast. (5) _____

your weekend was OK after that?

Ray: Yeah, I guess it was OK in the end. We took the dog for a walk in the park and had a picnic. How about you? How was your weekend?

B. Your Turn

Roleplay the conversation with a partner. How would Ali answer the last question?

Your idea: _____

_____

 C. Listen to the audio and take notes. Prepare to respond and react to what your partner says.

Pair and Share

Practice reacting to what your partner says. Then change roles.

You look happy today!

Yes, I *am* happy . . .

How was your weekend?

It was . . .

Reading Strategy:
Infer the author's intentions

- Read a text and try to make inferences about the author's intentions.
- Ask, *Why did he / she write this?*
- Find clues in the text.

Before Reading

A. Look at the pictures and discuss the question.
What good deeds do you think these girls have done?

B. Read the text and underline the good deeds.

 A Thousand Good Deeds: The Story of Grace Campbell

Some people's lives are an example to us all. Take Grace Campbell, an American teenager who **tries** to do a good deed every day, for example. Most of what she does are small actions, like holding a door open, listening to a friend who has a problem, or cleaning the sidewalk in front of a neighbor's house. Grace says young people can change the world with one good deed at a time. She believes that small deeds help bring a neighborhood or a town **together.** "If we help neighbors in need, more people will be friends".

Grace was inspired by her mother, who always did good deeds. One of Grace's friends told us that they were at a restaurant, and the food was cheaper than Grace expected. She then gave 20 dollars to the server to pay for an older couple's lunch. The friend asked why Grace did this, and Grace answered that it was a nice thing to do. Another day, Grace was waiting in **line** at a store. She stepped out of the line to get a cup of coffee for herself . . . and the person behind her in the line.

Grace **realized** that these small actions can have an impact on people's lives. She then **planned** to do more good deeds. She started a plan called "1,000 Good Deeds." She couldn't do 1,000 good deeds in a year on her own, so she **decided** to ask others for help. First she **contacted** her Girl Scouts organization to **promote** the program, then her school, and a few other places. Later, in high school, she joined a program called Peer Buddies.

Grace promotes the idea of "paying it forward." This means that when somebody does something nice for you, you respond by doing a good deed for someone else.

If everybody "pays it forward" like Grace, the world will be a better place.

After Reading

C. Number the events in the order they happened.

_____ Grace started "1,000 Good Deeds."

_____ Grace bought coffee for a stranger.

_____ Grace was inspired by her mother.

_____ joined Peer Buddies.

D. In pairs, discuss these questions.

1. Grace feels the need to help others. Why?

2. Why does Grace promote "paying it forward"?

3. What are the author's intentions? Find sentences in the text.

---

8 | Writing

**Writing Strategy:
Write a short story**

- Start by introducing the main character.
- Then introduce the problem.
- Finally, give the solution.

A. Choose one of the stories from this unit. Write notes about the main character, his / her problem, and the solution he / she found.

B. Think about a selfless person you know and write notes in the chart below.

Selfless heroes		
	Example	**My hero**
Character	Michael Bowron 8 years old really brave	
Problem	road accident in the desert his father couldn't move	
Solution	connected radio to a battery called for help	

C. Write your hero's story.

Example: Michael Bowron was only eight years old, but he was really brave. He was with his father, who was driving a truck in a desert in Australia. They had an accident and his father couldn't move. Michael found the radio and connected it to a battery. Then he called the ambulance and they were rescued.

ABC Vocabulary

A. Complete the sentences using the verbs from the box.

believed	**died**	**hasn't improved**
promoted	**tried**	**wished**

Flower Power

The flower power movement was a symbol of antiviolence in the U.S. and other places around the world. The "flower children" (1) _____ peace. They liked to wear clothes with flowers in vibrant colors.

They never had an official organization. The individuals (2) _____ to be kind to others. They often gave flowers to soldiers, because many people (3) _____ in wars. The flower children (4) _____ for the end of violence. They (5) _____ they could change the world. Unfortunately, the situation (6) _____ much: there is still violence and crime in many countries.

B. Circle the correct word.

Generosity is the act of being 1. (brave / generous), not selfish. Generous people give attention, time, or money to people in 2. (line / need), especially people who are suffering in 3. (poverty / respect) or from a serious 4. (illness / rescue).

Charitable organizations 5. (plan / wish) large projects, but people can do small good deeds, too. Anyone can 6. (decide / need) to be more generous and 7. (kind / together) to others.

C. Match the words to the correct definitions.

1. improve	• •	a kind act that you do for someone
2. poverty	• •	courageous
3. violence	• •	save someone or something from a dangerous situation
4. favor	• •	a story of a person's life
5. biography	• •	the state of being poor
6. brave	• •	make better
7. rescue	• •	behavior that hurts someone or damages things

Grammar

A. Write questions using the words below. Then answer them.

1. go swimming / tomorrow / will

    _____

2. do the shopping / today / going to

    _____

3. visit your grandmother / soon / will

    _____

4. watch a movie / on Saturday / going to

    _____

B. Match the sentence parts.

1. Is •	•	should help her then.
2. We •	•	your mother sick?
3. Let's •	•	give it to her today?
4. I'd like •	•	do the shopping for her.
5. Could you •	•	to write her a get-well card.

C. Complete the sentences using the pronouns in parentheses.

1. (me, you) I finished that exercise already. Do _____ want _____ to help you?

2. (he, her) Samuel's sister can bake delicious cookies. _____ 's going to ask _____ to bake some this afternoon.

3. (him, you) Will you see our history teacher today? Could _____ ask _____ if we can hand in the report on Monday?

4. (her, them) Sally wants to go the basketball game, but I can't take her today. Ashley's parents are going to the game, too. I can ask _____ to give _____ a lift.

 Reading: Environmental Studies

 Global Warming

What is global warming?

The term "global warming" indicates that the temperatures on Earth are rising. Global warming causes changes in the Earth's atmosphere, leading to floods and hurricanes.

There are people that say Earth has always had warm and cold periods. According to this theory, global warming is not something that is caused by humans, and we cannot change it. However, many governments and **organizations** around the world are convinced that global warming is a man-made event and it should be stopped. The reason for global warming is carbon dioxide (CO_2) in the air caused by deforestation and the burning of fossil fuels (mainly oil and gas). The CO_2 levels in the atmosphere are the highest they have been in thousands of years.

If we don't stop global warming, many plants and animals will **die** off. Some land areas will turn into deserts, and other places will disappear into the ocean. These changes will make it very difficult—or impossible—to grow food for Earth's population. Access to clean water will become a problem, too. Is there any way we can **improve** things?

How to stop global warming

• Take a shower instead of a bath. That saves lots of water!
• **Promote** recycling and separation of garbage in your home.
• Reuse! Reuse your shopping bag or take a cloth bag with you to the supermarket.
• Take a lunch box, not plastic bags.
• Ask your parents to buy local fruits and vegetables. This saves the amount of fuel used for transportation.

A. Read the sentences and circle T for *True* or F for *False*. Correct the false statements.

1. Everybody in the world agrees that climate change is happening.   T   F

_____

2. The reason for global warming is high levels of CO_2 in the atmosphere.   T   F

_____

3. Global warming can cause some plants and animals to disappear.   T   F

_____

4. It is the government's responsibility to reduce CO_2 levels.   T   F

_____

B. Put these ideas in the order they appear in the text.

1. _____ It will be hard to grow food.

2. _____ CO_2 levels in the atmosphere have increased.

3. _____ Global warming is a man-made event.

4. _____ Don't use plastic bags.

5. _____ We can't change global warming.

6. _____ Earth's temperatures are rising.

C. With a classmate, discuss what you can do to stop global warming. Write notes.

_____

_____

_____

_____

D. Write some things you and your family could do to stop global warming. Explain your answers.

_____

_____

_____

_____

E. Share your notes with your classmates. Make a bar graph and decide which actions are less possible and which are more possible to do.

 **Project**

In this project, you will make a PowerPoint®
presentation of a story. Use what you know from
Units 10 to 12 to complete the project.

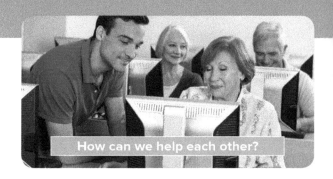

How can we help each other?

Step 1   Research

Find a story about someone helping others. Go on the Internet to look for stories or ask people you know.
Write details about the story below.

Step 2   Create

Make a PowerPoint presentation of your story. Use images. Don't use too much text.

Step 3   Rehearse

Practice your presentation. Let a classmate
give you some feedback.

Step 4   Present

Present your project to the class.

Creative Zone

Planning

A. Work in pairs. Research a charitable organization in your city. Describe what they do.

_____

_____

_____

_____

_____

_____

B. Work in groups. Compare the organizations.

1. Discuss: How are the organizations similar? How are they different?
2. Choose one organization that you could help. Prepare a presentation about that organization. If necessary, go online or visit the place to get more information.

Presentation

C. Work with the whole class.

1. Listen to each group's presentations.
2. Choose one organization to visit as a class and do some volunteer work.

Wh- Questions

Question	Answer
Who is she?	She is my mother.
What are you doing?	I am watching a movie.
Where do they live?	They live in Tokyo.
When is your English class?	It's from 3 to 4 o'clock.
Why is he not here?	He is in school now.
How are they doing?	They are doing fine.
Which one do you like?	I like the blue one.

Want to

Use *to* + verb after the verb ***want*** to mean *"wish for or desire something."*

Subject	Want	Infinitive	Complement
I	want	to do	the dishes.
You	want	to wash	your hands.
She	wants	to paint	her bedroom.
He	wants	to go	to the mall.
We	want	to buy	some vegetables.
They	want	to clean	the house.

Yes / No Questions with the verb *Be*

Yes / No Questions		
Is the flag white, red, blue, and black?	Yes, it is.	No, it isn't.
Are there any celebrations in July in your city?	Yes, there are.	No, there aren't.

Count and Noncount Nouns with *some / any / a / an*

Use *a / an* for singular count nouns and *some / any* for plural count nouns.

Singular	Plural
Linda is lighting **a** candle. He has **an** egg every morning.	There are **some** flowers on the table. There aren't **any** oranges in the basket.

Use *some* with count nouns and noncount nouns in affirmative sentences.

Use *any* with count nouns and noncount nouns in questions and negative sentences.

Use *some* in questions when you offer or ask for something.

	some	any
Affirmative	I picked **some** apples. She made **some** tea for us.	--
Negative	--	My sister didn't get **any** presents. There isn't **any** bread left.
Question	Would you like **some** tea? Can I have **some** sugar?	Are there **any apples** left for the cake? Is there **any money** to buy more decorations?

Questions with *How often*

Question	Answer
How often do you make your bed?	I make my bed **every day.**
How often does he go swimming?	He goes swimming **once a week.**
How often does Mary practice the piano?	She practices the piano **twice a week.**
How often do they go to see a movie?	They go to see a movie **three times a month.**
How often do we take a test?	We take a test **four times a year.**

Adverbs of Frequency

Subject	Adverb	Verb	Complement
I	**always**	make	my bed.
My mom	**usually / normally**	makes	a sandwich for me.
We	**sometimes**	wash	the dishes together.
My brother	**never**	cleans	the bathroom.

Know how to vs *Learn how to*

Know how to means someone has practiced something and has the ability to do it well. ***Learn how to*** means someone is new at something and does *not* have the ability to do it well.

*Rahul **knows how to play** soccer. He has played soccer for 10 years.*

*Rahul's brother **learns how to play** soccer on Saturdays. He wants to become good at it.*

Simple Past with *be* and Other Verbs

Verb *be*	Subject	Complement
Was	money	important to you?
Were	they	late for school?

Subject	Verb *be*	Complement
I	**was**	a young man once.
Things	**were**	important to me then.
He	**wasn´t**	happy.
We	**weren´t**	ready to leave.

Question word	Auxiliary (helping) verb: *did*	Subject	Verb	Complement
What	**did**	you	**learn?**	
–	**Did**	you	**have**	many gadgets?

Subject	Verb in past	Complement
I	**learned**	something about myself.
My family	**had**	a good time.

Subject	Auxiliary (helping) verb: *didn't*	Verb	Complement
I	**didn't**	**need**	gadgets.
We	**didn't**	**have**	cell phones.

There was / There were

There was / were	Complement
There was / wasn't	a lot of traffic.
There were / weren't	many cars.
Was there	a party?
Were there	many people?

Indefinite Pronouns

Indefinite pronouns include *someone, nothing, no one, anything.* These words don't refer to any specific thing or person.

Pronoun / Subject	Verb	Complement
Someone / No one	planted	a tree in our street.

Subject	Verb	Pronoun / Object
We	saw	**nothing.**
We	**did *not* see**	**anything.**

Used to

The expression **used to** indicates an action in the past that a person doesn't do anymore in the present.

Subject	Used to	Verb	Complement
I	**used to**	spend	a lot of time with my friends.
She	**didn't use to**	sing	so well.

Should / Shouldn't

Should and **shouldn't** are used to give advice or make a recommendation.

Question Word	Should	Subject	Verb	Complement
What	**should**	I	do	to be more understanding?
	Should	we	share	our ideas and feelings?

Subject	Should	Verb	Complement
You	**should**	listen	when someone talks to you.
You	**shouldn't**	criticize	a person's opinion.

Imperatives

Imperatives can also be used to give advice.

Verb	Complement
Enjoy	middle school first.
Don't try	to grow up so fast.

Should

Should expresses a recommendation. For a negative recommendation, use **shouldn't**.

Subject	Should	Verb	Complement
We	**should**	**get**	passport pictures.
You	**shouldn't**	**eat**	unsafe food.

Should	Subject	Verb	Complement
Should	I	**buy**	plane tickets online?
Should	we	**work**	together on this project?

Have to / Had to

Have to is used to indicate an obligation in the present. **Had to** is used to indicate an obligation in the past.

Subject	Have to / Had to	Verb	Complement
Jim	**has to**	**do**	a lot of homework today.
I	**had to**	**walk**	to school fast. I was late!

Auxiliary	Subject	Have to	Complement
Do	you	have to	pack your own suitcase?
Does	Simone	have to	wake up at 6:30?
Did	you	have to	be home early?

Possessive Adjectives and Possessive Pronouns

Possessive adjectives and possessive pronouns both show ownership—who something belongs to. Possessive adjectives go before a noun. Possessive pronouns replace the possessive adjective and the noun.

Possessive adjective	Possessive pronoun
It's **my** dog.	It's **mine**.
It's **your** dog.	It's **yours**.
It's **his** dog.	It's **his**.
It's **her** dog.	It's **hers**.
It's **our** dog.	It's **ours**.
It's **your** dog.	It's **yours**.
It's **their** dog.	It's **theirs**.

Whose

The question word for possession is ***whose***:

Whose *book is this? It's mine. / It's Julia's. / It's hers.*

Pronouns: *One / Ones*

Use the pronouns ***one*** and ***ones*** to refer to objects that were mentioned before. *One* is used in singular and *ones* in plural.

*I broke my glasses, so I'll have to buy some new **ones**.*

*There are two books on the table. The **one** on the right is mine.*

Too + adjective

Use the adverb ***too*** + adjective to describe that something is excessive. This structure usually expresses a negative idea.

*These jeans are **too big**. (They don't fit me.)*

*The ice cream is **too expensive**. (I don't have the money.)*

Comparatives

Descriptive adjectives are used to make comparisons. When the word *than* is used, the form of the adjective changes.

• Use *-er* for most one-syllable adjectives (except *more ill* and *more fun*).

• Use *more* before the adjective for most two- or more syllable adjectives (except *quieter* and *cleverer*).

Adjective	Comparison in a sentence
new	Your backpack is **newer than** mine.
fast	A plane is **faster than** a car.
interesting	I think basketball is **more interesting than** baseball.
fashionable	That dress is **more fashionable than** jeans and a blouse.

Superlatives

The superlative is formed with *-est* or *most*.

The rules for superlative forms are similar to the rules for comparatives.

Adjective	Superlative in a sentence
new	This band's **newest** song is incredible!
interesting	I think *Animal Farm* was Orwell's **most interesting** book.

Spelling changes with comparatives and superlatives

Double the consonant for short adjectives ending in consonant + vowel + consonant:

*bi**g** > bi**gg**er, bi**gg**est*   *ho**t** > ho**tt**er, ho**tt**est*

Adjectives ending in *-y* change to *-ier* in the comparative form, and to *-iest* in superlatives:

*happ**y** > happ**ier**, happ**iest***   *eas**y** > eas**ier**, eas**iest***

Add an *-r* in comparatives and *-st* in superlatives for adjectives that end in *-e*.

*nic**e** > nic**er**, nic**est***   *larg**e** > larg**er**, larg**est***

Irregular comparatives and superlatives

Some adjectives do not follow the rules above. They are completely irregular.

bad > worse, worst   *far > farther, farthest*
good > better, best   *many > more, most*

Will for future actions

The auxiliary **will** is used to talk about future actions. The form *will* is the same for all persons: *I will play, she will listen, they will learn*. The negative form is **won't**.

	Examples
affirmative	He **will invite** his friends to his karaoke party next Friday.
negative	They **won't sing** songs in English.
questions	**Will** you **bake** a cake, or **will** you **buy** one?
question words	What time **will** the party **start**?

Be going to to express future

The structure **be + going to** + verb can be used to talk about something that will happen in the future.

	Examples
affirmative	We**'re going to register** for the recycling campaign. We**'re** all **going to bring in** recyclable materials.
negative	We **aren't going to collect** money.
questions	**Are** you **going to donate** the materials?
question words	Where **are you going to take** them?

Will vs *Going to*

In general, **will** and **going to** can be used interchangeably. However, they can also express different intentions.

Use *will*:

• for predictions: *It **will get** colder over the next days.*

• for promises or spontaneous decisions: *I**'ll help** you.*

• to express desire or preference: ***Will** you **come** to my party?*

Use *going to*:

• to express planned actions and decisions: *We**'re going to visit** Australia this December.*

• to describe what you are sure is going to happen: *Jon**'s going to tell** jokes at the party.*

• when you see something about to happen: *It**'s going to rain**.*

Can / Could for possibility

The modal **can** is used to make general statements about possible things.

Example: *We **can walk** around downtown at night; it's very safe.*

Could is the past tense of can.

Example: ***Could** you **get** on the train this morning?*

Could is also used to show that something might happen in the future.

Example: *If we don't leave now, we **could be** late for the show.*

Want / Tell / Ask for requests

The pattern to use when making and talking about requests is:

want / tell / ask + the object + infinitive verb form

Subject	Want / tell / ask	Object	Infinitive	Complement
His brother	**wanted**	me	to lend	him some money.
The teacher	**told**	us (the students)	to study	for the test.
Hu	**asked**	her (his mom)	to prepare	his dinner early.

Let / Will to show intentions

Let me and **I'll** are used to express intention to do something immediately.

Intention	Verb	Complement
Let me	open	the door for you.
I'll	buy	them a nice present.

Simple Past

The **simple past** tense expresses an action that began and finished at a definite time in the past.

Subject	Past Tense Verb	Complement
I	**played**	football last Saturday.
Jimena	**wasn't**	at school yesterday.
We	**paid**	in cash at 9 a.m.

The simple past uses the auxiliary *did:*

• in questions

Did you **have** *a good time at the party?*

Did *your friends **dance** a lot?*

• in the negative form

*Erin **didn't have** any problems finding the address.*

*The Watsons **didn't like** the food at the new restaurant very much.*

The verb *be* is an exception.

Present Perfect

In the negative form, we add *not* to *have*.

The word *yet* indicates that the person is planning to do it, but hasn't done the action.

Subject	Auxiliary	Verb in past participle	Complement
Diane	**hasn't**	**called**	her parents (yet).
We	**haven't**	**seen**	that movie (yet).

Present Perfect vs Simple Past

We use **present perfect** when we don't know when an action happened, or when an action started and is still going on. We use **simple past** for an action that started and finished in the past.

*The Robson family **has visited** the capital once this year.*

(We don't know when the action happened.)

*They **went** to the capital last February.*

(We know when the action happened.)

Vocabulary Lists

Module 1

1	closet	clothing	different	dining room
	gather	kitchen	prepare	privacy
	same	wall	warm	window

2	barbecue	birthday	celebrate	Christmas
	decorate	festival	flag	holiday
	Independence Day	Mother's Day	New Year	organize

3	always	arrive	clean up	go
	make	make dinner	never	normally
	sometimes	take	take a selfie/a picture	usually

Module 2

4	ago	apartment	daughter	do your best
	job	last	late	make someone happy
	sneakers	stuff	teenager	yesterday

5	change	cheap	exist	get-together
	impossible	mall	market	meet
	meeting point	problem	quickly	research

6	accept	advice	behave	embarrassed
	give up	hygiene	judge	nice
	no big deal	shy	sociable	take a shower

Vocabulary Lists

Module 3

7	abroad	capital	distance	explore
	fast	foreign	passport	safe
	slowly	suitcase	trip	visa

8	add	cheap	collect	compare
	expensive	grow up	include	keep
	prefer	price	rare	show

9	airline	backpack	best	comfortable
	common	cost	cruise	easy
	incredible	passenger	suitable	view

Module 4

10	believe	community	generous	happiness
	improve	kind	necessary	need
	organization	recently	respect	useful

11	crime	death	die	ecology
	favor	illness	peace	poverty
	request	sick	violence	wish

12	biography	brave	contact	decide
	hurt	line	plan	promote
	realize	rescue	together	try

Audio Tracks

Track	Unit	Section
1	Unit 1	Get Ready: Activity A
2	Unit 1	Vocabulary: Activity A
3	Unit 1	Vocabulary: Word Box
4	Unit 1	Listening: Activity B
5	Unit 1	Pronunciation: Activity A
6	Unit 1	Pronunciation: Activity B
7	Unit 1	Conversation: Activity A
8	Unit 1	Conversation: Activity C
9	Unit 1	Reading: Activity B
10	Unit 2	Get Ready: Activity A
11	Unit 2	Vocabulary: Activity A
12	Unit 2	Vocabulary: Word Box
13	Unit 2	Listening: Activity B
14	Unit 2	Pronunciation: Activity A
15	Unit 2	Pronunciation: Activity B
16	Unit 2	Conversation: Activity A
17	Unit 2	Conversation: Activity C
18	Unit 2	Reading: Activity B
19	Unit 3	Get Ready: Activity A
20	Unit 3	Get Ready: Activity B
21	Unit 3	Vocabulary: Activity A
22	Unit 3	Vocabulary: Word Box
23	Unit 3	Listening: Activity B
24	Unit 3	Pronunciation: Activity A
25	Unit 3	Pronunciation: Activity B
26	Unit 3	Conversation: Activity A
27	Unit 3	Conversation: Activity C
28	Unit 3	Reading: Activity B
29	Use What You Know: Units 1–3	Reading: CLIL
30	Unit 4	Get Ready: Activity A
31	Unit 4	Vocabulary: Activity A
32	Unit 4	Vocabulary: Word Box
33	Unit 4	Vocabulary: Activity C
34	Unit 4	Listening: Activity B
35	Unit 4	Pronunciation: Activity A
36	Unit 4	Pronunciation: Activity B
37	Unit 4	Conversation: Activity A
38	Unit 4	Conversation: Activity C
39	Unit 4	Reading: Activity B
40	Unit 5	Get Ready: Activity A
41	Unit 5	Vocabulary: Activity A

Audio Tracks

Track	Unit	Section
42	Unit 5	Vocabulary: Word Box
43	Unit 5	Vocabulary: Activity C
44	Unit 5	Listening: Activity B
45	Unit 5	Pronunciation: Activity A
46	Unit 5	Pronunciation: Activity B
47	Unit 5	Conversation: Activity A
48	Unit 5	Conversation: Activity C
49	Unit 5	Reading: Activity B
50	Unit 6	Get Ready: Activity A
51	Unit 6	Vocabulary: Activity A
52	Unit 6	Vocabulary: Word Box
53	Unit 6	Vocabulary: Activity C
54	Unit 6	Listening: Activity B
55	Unit 6	Pronunciation: Activity A
56	Unit 6	Pronunciation: Activity B
57	Unit 6	Conversation: Activity A
58	Unit 6	Conversation: Activity C
59	Unit 6	Reading: Activity B
60	Use What You Know: Unit 4–6	Reading: CLIL
61	Unit 7	Get Ready: Activity A
62	Unit 7	Vocabulary: Activity A
63	Unit 7	Vocabulary: Word Box
64	Unit 7	Listening: Activity B
65	Unit 7	Pronunciation: Activity A
66	Unit 7	Pronunciation: Activity B
67	Unit 7	Conversation: Activity A
68	Unit 7	Conversation: Activity C
69	Unit 7	Reading: Activity B
70	Unit 8	Get Ready: Activity A
71	Unit 8	Vocabulary: Activity A
72	Unit 8	Vocabulary: Word Box
73	Unit 8	Listening: Activity B
74	Unit 8	Pronunciation: Activity A
75	Unit 8	Pronunciation: Activity B
76	Unit 8	Conversation: Activity A
77	Unit 8	Conversation: Activity C
78	Unit 8	Reading: Activity B
79	Unit 9	Get Ready: Activity A
80	Unit 9	Vocabulary: Activity A
81	Unit 9	Vocabulary: Word Box
82	Unit 9	Listening: Activity B

Audio Tracks

Track	Unit	Section
83	Unit 9	Pronunciation: Activity A
84	Unit 9	Pronunciation: Activity B
85	Unit 9	Conversation: Activity A
86	Unit 9	Conversation: Activity C
87	Unit 9	Reading: Activity B
88	Use What You Know: Units 7–9	Reading: CLIL
89	Unit 10	Get Ready: Activity A
90	Unit 10	Get Ready: Activity B
91	Unit 10	Vocabulary: Activity A
92	Unit 10	Vocabulary: Word Box
93	Unit 10	Listening: Activity B
94	Unit 10	Listening: Activity C
95	Unit 10	Pronunciation: Activity A
96	Unit 10	Pronunciation: Activity B
97	Unit 10	Conversation: Activity A
98	Unit 10	Conversation: Activity C
99	Unit 10	Reading: Activity B
100	Unit 11	Get Ready: Activity A
101	Unit 11	Vocabulary: Activity A
102	Unit 11	Vocabulary: Word Box
103	Unit 11	Vocabulary: Activity B
104	Unit 11	Listening: Activity B
105	Unit 11	Pronunciation: Activity A
106	Unit 11	Pronunciation: Activity B
107	Unit 11	Conversation: Activity A
108	Unit 11	Conversation: Activity C
109	Unit 11	Reading: Activity B
110	Unit 12	Get Ready: Activity A
111	Unit 12	Get Ready: Activity B
112	Unit 12	Vocabulary: Activity A
113	Unit 12	Vocabulary: Word Box
114	Unit 12	Listening: Activity B
115	Unit 12	Pronunciation: Activity A
116	Unit 12	Pronunciation: Activity B
117	Unit 12	Conversation: Activity A
118	Unit 12	Conversation: Activity C
119	Unit 12	Reading: Activity B
120	Use What You Know: Units 10–12	Reading: CLIL

Photo Credits